DESIGN IN B

Botanical Craft Projects

Every Occasion

SANDU

DESIGN IN BLOOM

Botanical Craft Projects For
Every Occasion

Sponsored by Design 360°
– Concept and Design Magazine

Edited and produced by
Sandu Publishing Co., Ltd.

Book design, concepts & art direction by
Sandu Publishing Co., Ltd.
Chief Editor: Wang Shaoqiang

info@sandupublishing.com
www.sandupublishing.com
weibo.com/sandupublishing
weibo.com/design360

Published by Sandu Publishing Co., Ltd.

Size: 185mm x 250mm
First Edition: 2015

Front cover project by Gloribell Lebron

ISBN 978-988-13582-5-7

Printed and bound in China

THE POWER OF THE PETAL

"Happiness held is the seed; Happiness shared is the flower." – John Harrigan.

What is it about the flower that catches our fancy?

Nature's ultimate decoration has come to symbolize many things to us – from showing signs of love, adoration, thanks, gratitude, condolences and, with the early seventies slogan of Flower Power, even peace.

Whether seeing spring's first blooms, forest floors lined with wood anemones, wild meadows bursting with poppies and cornflowers, or a bright harebell nestled amongst craggy stones beach-side, the surprise and delight of flowers enthralls and entices.

Flowers brighten moods, adding color and cheer. They sit places of pride, bringing the outside in to restore our spirits and add a natural decorative touch.

Mother Nature's beautiful offerings have also inspired a legion of writers, artists and crafters to create their own works, mirroring the beauty of nature in each interpretation.

Poets and authors have written and mused over the flower for centuries. The beauty of women has been compared to that of a flower, and the delicacies and intricacies of love paralleled. Some of the world's most valuable and esteemed artworks have includedobservations of flowers – from Monet's water lilies, to Van Gogh's Sunflowers, Warhol's Ten-Foot Flowers, and the abstract hyper-real sculptures from Yayoi Kusama.

Springing up amongst this are the legions of crafters with an enthusiasm for décor – all ardent fans of the flower.

With a do-it-yourself approach to recreating nature's art, whether through baking brilliance, paper prowess or the finest of fabrics, crafters are making and sharing their floral creations for all to follow and reproduce.

This book celebrates the power of the petal and the creativity of crafting, from the everyday flower DIY, to those special celebratory occasions, showing you how to use simple techniques and materials to make stunning decorations.

The pages of *Design in Bloom* include over 60 DIY projects from more than 40 designers the world over.

The projects span from fresh flower creations to dried and even edible projects, mixing materials such as paper, felt, clay and silk to showcase the most unique and easy to follow guides, with precise photos to help explain the steps.

From The House That Lars Built and her gorgeous Valentine's paper floral crown, to delicious cake pop rose buds from CakeGirls, paper bouquets by Lia Griffiths, and the most realistic of potted paper succulents from Craftberry Bush, the following pages are in full bloom with all manner of petal and plant projects.

From festivals, food and drink, centerpieces, to wedding bouquets, flower crowns and many more, flowers are applied skillfully for your decorative delight.

These pages will inspire you to get your craft on, to celebrate nature's finest forms, and plant your own seed of flower DIY decorating and make your crafting skills flourish.

We want to see what you make, so post your pictures on Instagram and #DesigninBloomDIY

Enjoy!

Knot & Pop

Fresh Flower Pendant Light

Crafting: Brittni Mehlhoff
Photography: Brittni Mehlhoff

This DIY flower pendant light project would be great for a dinner party, especially once the holidays start rolling around. The idea was to create something that would act as a centerpiece without getting in the way of conversation or take up too much space (or any space at all) on a smaller dining table.

Materials:

• Fresh flowers and greenery

• Large wire basket with a hole at the bottom that your light kit will fit through

• Hanging light kit

• Light bulb

• Floral tape

• Floral wire

How-To:

1. Flip your basket over so the bottom is facing up. This is the framework for your pendant lampshade. Now you're ready to begin.

2. You'll want to start with the greenery (like Green Pittisporum) as your base. Cut off decent size sprigs (6-10") from a larger branch and begin attaching them to the wire basket with floral wire. You can also weave some of the pieces in and out of the basket for extra security. For heavy stems or branches, use heavy gauge wire.

3. Start weaving some of the other greenery into the frame at this time as well (like Viburnum berries).

4. Attach some blooms as a finishing touch.

5. Once your pendant is complete, string the cord of your light kit through the hole in the basket and screw in the light bulb.

Floral Heart Backdrop

Floral Design: Janelle Nicole Wylie of Lavenders Flowers
Photography: Joel Maus of Studio EMP Photography
Creative Direction: Lorely Meza

Materials:

• Chicken wire

• Clippers

• Staple gun

• 2 found pieces of wood

• 2 buckets

• Sand

• Forged seasonal florals such as willow eucalyptus, bougainvillea, jasmine, and pepper tree

How-To:

1. Spread out the chicken wire to desired width and cut with clippers.

2. Staple chicken wire to found wood.

3. Secure chicken wire structure in the sand filled buckets.

4. Begin weaving the largest green (willow eucalyptus) in the desired shape. For this shoot we made a heart.

5. Continue re-enforcing the heart shape with the next largest green (here, pepper tree clippings).

6. Continue adding greens as needed. To get a natural, earthy feel, add jasmine at the base of the structure coming out of the sand and wrap it around the wood pieces.

7. Fill the heart in with the bougainvillea blooms. This gives it a nice pop of color and really brings out the shape of the heart.

Floral Party Place Setting

Crafting: Brittni Mehlhoff
Photography: Brittni Mehlhoff

The best part of throwing any dinner party is planning the decorating details.

Remind guests to 'have a ball' at your next sit down get-together with these unique, rope ball place settings. Adorned with fresh flowers and a handwritten place card, guests will feel welcome from the minute they grab their seat at the table.

Materials:

- Air plants or small florals that can survive without much water

- Scissors

- Craft glue

- Paper mache ball (or tennis ball)

- Floral wire

- Wire cutters

- Upholstery piping cord

How-To:

1. Glue one end of your upholstery cord to the paper mache ball and let it dry. Once dry, begin wrapping the cord around the ball until it is almost completely covered.

2. When the ball is mostly concealed by the cord, it is time to start adding flowers. Place the flowers one at a time and cover the stems with the cord as you continue to wrap the cord around and around the ball.

3. Continue this process until you have reached the desired look. Cut off any excess cord and glue the end of the cord to the ball.

4. Cut a long piece of floral wire that can be formed into a coil. Use this as a stand for your rope ball in. It will rest inside this coil, without rolling away.

Add a handwritten place card and an extra bloom or two and you have a unique place setting that will make your guests smile.

Your guests can take these home at the end of the night, while the flowers are still fresh, to use as decoration in their homes. Great for weddings too!

Leaf Candle Holder

Design: Dani Altamura
Crafting: Dani Altamura
Photography: Dani Altamura

Materials:

• Leaves of various shapes and sizes

• Small glass tumblers

• Double sided tape

• Scissors

• Twine/String

• Tea light candles

Maybe it's autumn where you are and the trees and leaves are in lovely warm hues. Perhaps, it's summer and everything is green and bright. Even if it's already coming into winter in your part of the world, you can use this wonderfully simple DIY project to bring a little bit of the outdoors in! Collect some pretty leaves and twigs from around your garden or neighborhood and you can put together these pretty little candle holders to decorate your home.

How-To:

1. Collect some leaves/branches from your garden to use. You want leaves that are as tall as your glass and flexible so that they can wrap around the glass without breaking. Separate the leaves from the branches and sort into groups. Three different sets of leaves are used in the images shown here – tall stems for a base, long thin leaves and pretty seeded "flowers" as decoration.

2. Run a line of double sided tape around the outside of glass about 1/3 of the way down from the top and just above the base of the glass.

3. Starting from one side, press the first base leaf onto the tape. Repeat with another leaf, overlapping the first. Continue all the way around the glass until you have covered the surface completely. It doesn't matter if you can see the glass through the leaves.

4. Take a length of twine or string that is at least twice as long as the diameter of the glass. Leaving around 2" (5 cm) at the end, use your thumb to anchor the string and start to layer the decoration leaves on top of the base row, using the string to anchor the new leaves. Continue around the glass until you are back at the beginning. This can be a little tricky, so try using a table to steady your hand.

5. Tie off the twine (using the 2" end you left in the previous step) and adjust any of the leaves that may have slipped in the process. Wrap the rest of the twine around the glass and tuck the end into the other row of twine.

6. Place a single tea light candle into each glass and light up to admire the pretty dappled light that flickers from between the leaves.

What's great about this project is that it's temporary. Your leaves will eventually break down and when they do, you can easily remove the string and tape and reclaim your glass tumblers to use as drinking glasses again.

Party Hats

Floral Design: Pollen Floral Design
DIY: Pollen Floral Design
Photography: Cambria Grace Photography
Concept: Lauren Wells Events
Styling: Lauren Wells Events

How-To:

1. Assemble the party hat.

2. Clip off all flower stems, so only flower heads remain.

3. Using the hot glue gun, place a dollop of glue on a flower head, and then place the flower on the hat. Continue placing flowers on the hat one by one.

4. Use a mixture of smaller blooms to fill in the spaces between the larger flowers.

5. The flowers will begin to wilt quickly after your hat is assembled. You can place your hat in the refrigerator to help them last longer. For best results, make your hat an hour or two before you plan to wear it.

6. Celebrate!

Fresh Flower Ring

Crafting: Brittni Mehlhoff
Photography: Brittni Mehlhoff

Using short-stemmed (or broken-stemmed) flowers that you would otherwise have to toss, try making a quick and easy fresh flower ring instead. It's a great way to dress up an outfit for a night out with friends or a summery picnic in the park.

Materials:

• Ring blank

• Glue gun

• Small flowers (like mums that will last a couple of days without water)

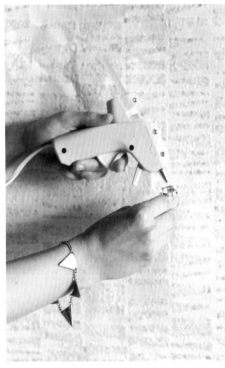

How-To:

1. Cut the stem completely off from the bloom.

2. Grab a ring blank, which you can find in the jewelry section at any craft store, and a glue gun. Add some hot glue to the ring.

3. Gently press the flower into the glue. Let it dry for a few minutes. Then wear it out.

Asymmetrical Floral Headband

Design: Liz Inigo Jones/blueskyflowers
Crafting: Liz Inigo Jones/blueskyflowers
Styling: Louise Beukes/Bloved Weddings
Photography: Anneli Marinovich

Materials:

- 1 open Coral Charm peony
- 1 Pearl Avalanche rose
- 2-3 small peach rose heads/buds
- 2-3 stems ivory sweet peas
- Clear plastic head band
- Hot glue gun (and suitable tray or base for the gun to sit in)

How-To:

1. Decide on the ideal shape and size of your headband and choose flowers accordingly.

2. Cut the peony and large rose just beneath the heads. Leave the smaller rose heads and buds with a little stem.

3. Decide where you want the main feature flower to go and place a generous amount of glue on the headband. Press the cut end of the peony onto the glue and hold for a minute or so until the glue cools and sets.

4. Add a stem or two of sweet pea to one side of the peony and then continue with roses and more sweet peas on the other side.

5. This headband is very quick and easy to make and will be fine for a day or so, but the fresh flowers won't last much longer than that.

Alternative flower suggestions:

You can use any strong flower – roses, dahlias, chrysanthemums, gerberas – as the feature flower and then experiment with other flowers, foliage and ribbon to go with it. You needn't use expensive flowers – and using fake ones is even easier!

Floral Crown

Floral Design & DIY: Amy Bowley from Bo Boutique
Styling: Fine & Fleurie
Photography: Jen Wojcik Photography

Materials:

- A branch of fresh stripped willow
- Flowers
- Floral tape or twine
- Floral wire
- Floral scissors

How-To:

1. Select flowers that are appropriate to the size of crown that you want to make. You should also select flowers that will last well without water.

2. Strip the remaining leaves from your willow, and wrap the willow around your head to ensure the right fit. Wire the willow together to form a simple circlet. You can conceal this wire with floral tape or twine.

3. Cut each of the flower stems to roughly 1" in length. Attach 3.5" pieces of wire to the stems by wrapping the wire and stems together with floral tape. About 3" of wire should be left exposed. This not only covers any sharp wires but also protects the flowers, ensuring moisture is locked within the stems for as long as possible.

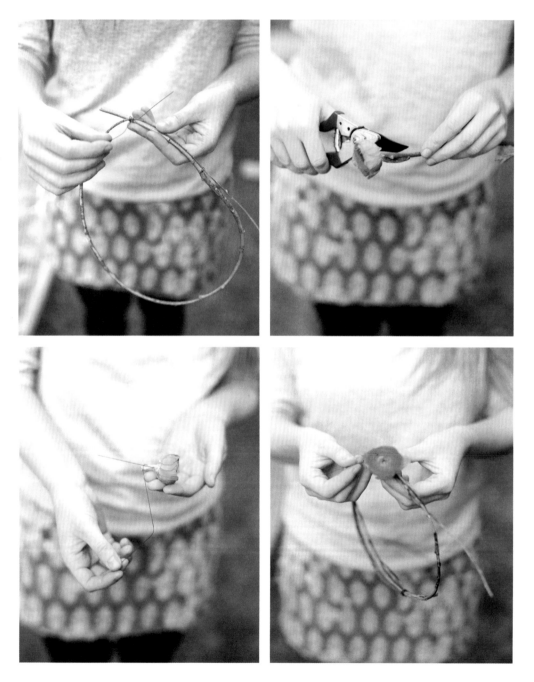

4. Place each flower in the desired spot on your circlet one by one. Wrap the wired part of the stem around the willow, so that each of the flowers is securely in place. Make sure that the flower heads are facing in the same direction and follow the shape of the circlet. You can be as experimental as you like with the size and the amount of flowers that you use. Asymmetrical crowns are lovely as they allow you to show off the natural beauty of both the willow and the flowers.

5. Voila! You have a beautiful, all natural crown!

Flower Jewelry

Design: By Madeline Trait
Crafting: By Madeline Trait
Photography: Caroline Winata

Materials:

• Flowers - Choose one to two larger blooms and two to three smaller flowers or foliage. Be creative and add dried seed pods, feathers, etc.

• Glue - Oasis Floral Adhesive and hot glue

• Ribbon - Approximately one yard

• Heavy fabric - Canvas or felt should work. You want something stiff that will hold its shape.

How-To:

1. Draw a semi circle shape that is 6" to 7" wide and not taller than 4". This will be the backing for your necklace, so try it on to make sure it is the right size to fit nicely just under your collar bone.

2. Cut your ribbon in two and tie it to the skinny ends of your fabric. To make sure it holds, add a drop of hot glue to the underside of the ribbon where it touches your fabric backing. This will be your "chain" for your necklace. (You can also make the ribbon longer and make a belt out of it or a dog collar for your best canine friend.)

3. Once you have your backing done, start laying out your flowers and other ingredients on your backing. When you are happy with how it looks, start gluing. Floral adhesive can get a bit messy, so you could try using a toothpick or small applicator. As you glue on your flowers and pods be sure to try it on every once in a while to make sure it lays correctly on your chest.

4. Give the flowers a quick spray with water, wrap and then deliver to your most fashion-forward friends. It can also be used as a headband or you can make a bracelet using the same technique. These should last about a day depending on the flowers you use. If they are flowers that dry nicely, you can dry them and keep it to wear all the time!

Mother's Day Floral Bangle Bracelet

Concept: Chelsea Foy of Lovely Indeed
Crafting: Chelsea Foy of Lovely Indeed
Photography: Chelsea Foy of Lovely Indeed
Tag Design: Lana Frankel of Lana's Shop

Make this sweet floral accessory for your
darling mom on Mother's Day, or any other
day of the year!

Materials:

• White cardstock

• Hole punch

• Baker's twine

• About 20 medium-sized blooms (ranunculus as examples)

• Floral wire

• Floral tape

• Scissors

047

How-To:

1. Make a card. You can draw or print whatever you like.

2. Punch a small hole in the card, and string it with ribbon or twine.

3. Start by taking the leaves and stems off of your blooms. Leave about 2-3 inches of stem.

4. Cut 30" of floral wire and form it into a circle large enough to fit on your mom's wrist like a bracelet. Wrap the wire around itself a few times to secure and strengthen the bracelet.

5. Begin attaching the blooms to the wire. Cut about 6" of floral tape, hold a stem against the wire, and wrap the tape around the base of the bloom and the wire. Continue the process around the wire, keeping the blooms close together and taping down the protruding stems as you go. Trim stems if needed.

6. Continue the process until you've covered the entire bracelet.

7. Gently tie on the tag and present it to your mom on Mother's Day!

i
LOVE
YOU
because...

you are
kind.

xoxo
s.

Wrist Corsage

Design: Karla Lim
Crafting: Karla Lim
Photography: Karla Lim

1. Select three shades of the same variety of flower as well as some fern to use as a base.

2. Get a pair of scissors or floral cutters.

3. Cut out two 2" diameter circles out of the felt sheet. This will be used as the base for the flowers.

4. Select a wireless gold ribbon. You'll need 24" per corsage.

5. Cut out a piece of wire and shape it into a half circle. This will help keep your corsage in place.

6. Turn on the hot glue gun, or prepare the floral adhesive. Wrap the ribbon around the wire, leaving equal lengths hanging on either side. Use the glue as needed to ensure the ribbon attaches well to the wire.

7. Now it's time to arrange the flowers. Arrange the fern on one of the felt circles and glue the stems in place.

8. Dab some glue onto the sides of the flowers and press them onto the felt circle in the desired arrangement.

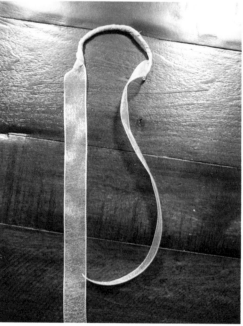

9. When you're done arranging and the glue has dried, turn the corsage on its back and glue your wristband onto the felt circle.

10. Glue the other felt circle onto the first one, so that the edges align and more of the wristband is covered.

11. Shape the wire around your wrist and secure the corsage by tying the ribbon into a pretty knot (or you can leave it hanging too!).

Buttonhole

Design: Lily & May
Crafting: Lily & May
Photography: Lily & May

Materials:

- Floral tape

- Twine

- Scissors

- Stub wire (The thickness will depend on the flowers used, for heavier flowers use thicker wire. 0.56mm and 0.32mm are used in this tutorial as the flowers are relatively light.)

- Mint leaves (Rosemary is another excellent herb for buttonholes.)

- Eucalyptus Cinerea

- Hypericum Berries

- Freesia

How-To:

1. Cut each stem to approximately 9 cm (you can always make this shorter at a later stage) and remove any unwanted leaves.

2. Each stem will now need to be wired. It is possible to place the materials together without this step, but it helps to strengthen delicate flowers and make the placement more flexible.

3. Take a 34 cm piece of wire and bend it at a right angle so that you have a 20 cm length and a 14 cm length.

4. Hold the flower between your thumb and index finger and position the wire so that the bend sits at the base of the bud and the 14 cm length rests parallel to the stem.

5. Wrap the 20 cm length around the stem and the 14 cm length. Continue wrapping down the 14 cm length.

6. Straighten the twisted wire when finished.

7. Repeat this process with all of your flower materials.

8. The next stage is to tape each wired stem. This not only helps to cover the wire but assists with locking moisture in.

9. Wrap a piece of floral tape around the top of the wire and flower stem. Twirl the stem while stretching and pulling the tape downward. The tape should be tightly wrapped around the wire and flower stem without any gaps.

10. Repeat the above process for each flower stem.

11. Now to place the flowers together. Start with your focal flower (usually the largest). In this instance the freesia is the focal.

12. Add all the flowers and herbs to the freesia by taping the stems together. Remember, this will be placed on a lapel, so all the flowers must face the same direction.

13. Once all the flower materials are securely taped together, cut the wired stems to the length required. Secure tape over the exposed wires so that no sharp ends can be seen.

14. Your buttonhole is now complete and ready to use. Add some twine for a finished look. The twine can be tired or wrapped around the stems.

Pressed Violas

Design: Erin Boyle for Gardenista
Photography: Erin Boyle for Gardenista

Pressed flowers have something of an old-fashioned air about them,
which is probably why people like them so much. The same delicacy
that makes violas and violets tricky as cut flowers makes them a
perfect option for pressing.

Materials:

· Violas

· An old book

· Parchment or wax paper

How-To:

1. Select violas with a bit of their leaves still attached. Gently pull off extra leaves until the stem has a shape that you think will be nice once pressed.

2. Open the book toward the back and place a sheet of parchment or wax paper over the page.

3. Lay your flowers face down on the parchment. After you have your flowers arranged the way you'd like, place the second piece of parchment on top of them.

4. Gently close the book. For thin flowers like violas or pansies, a week or ten days is all you really need to get a nice press.

5. After your flowers are dried, you can glue them to thank you notes or place cards as impressive embellishments.

fleur

Pressed Flower Greetings Card

Design: Lisa Murdoch
Crafting: Lisa Murdoch
Photography: Lisa Murdoch

Use wild flowers or the odd stem from any plant you have in your
home or garden. The carnation shown in this example had snapped
off from a larger stem and it seemed only right to rescue it. Press your
flowers in a book for about a week.

Materials:

- A pressed flower
- Plain card
- Washi tape
- Letter stamps and ink (optional)
- Scissors

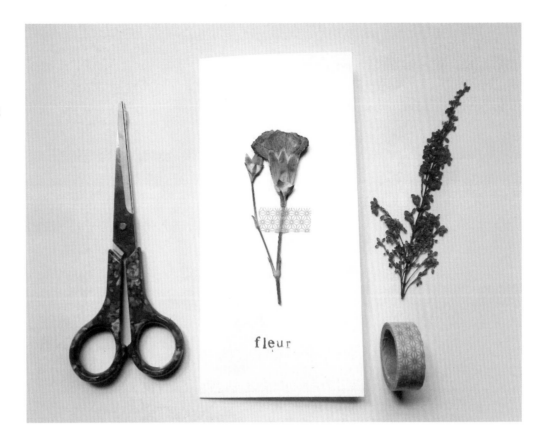

How-To:

1. Place your pressed flower in the center of your card stock.

2. Snip off a small piece of washi tape and secure the flower in place.

3. Depending on the occasion, stamp out any text you desire using alphabet stamps.

Floral Easter Eggs

Design: Whitney Curtis
Crafting: Whitney Curtis
Photography: Whitney Curtis

Materials:

- Flowers
- White eggs
- Paintbrush
- Mod Podge

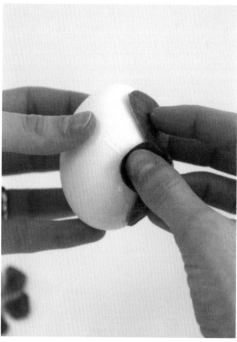

How-To:

1. You'll want to use the flattest flowers you have. Clip off the stem and any pollen tubes.

2. Use a paintbrush to coat the surface of your egg with Mod Podge, so the flower will stick to it.

3. Place the flower on the egg. Coat the flower in a layer of mod podge and wait for it to dry. The coating will be white when you paint it on, but will dry clear and shiny!

4. For pansies or any thicker flower, you might want to start by putting them in wax paper and slipping them between the pages of a thick book to flatten them. The pansies shown here were pressed for 24 hours and turned out perfectly.

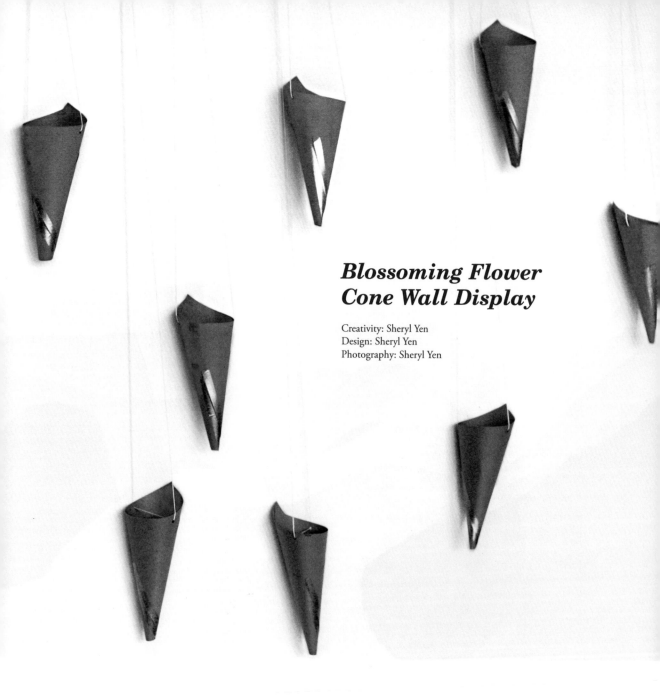

Blossoming Flower Cone Wall Display

Creativity: Sheryl Yen
Design: Sheryl Yen
Photography: Sheryl Yen

Materials:

• A few sheets of 8.5 x 11" cardstock
(each sheet makes 2 cones)

• Tape of any sort

• Hole punch

• String

• Cherry blossoms (or any other flower
you would like to use in your display)

How-To:

1. Cut each card stock sheet in half so that you have sheets that are 8.5 x 5.5".

2. Roll your sheets of cardstock into cones so that the center of one of the 8.5" sides becomes the tip of the cone.

3. Secure the cone by placing a strip of tape along the exposed loose edge of card stock, sealing it to the cone.

4. Punch two holes across from each other on the wide end of the cone.

5. Now take the string and cut it into pieces that will allow the cones to hang where you'd like. To do so, measure the distance from where you will anchor the string to where you would like the cones to hang. You'll need a little over twice as much string per cone.

6. Feed the string through both of the punched holes and hang the cone pointed side down.

7. Arrange the cones however you'd like. You can create a pattern or hang them so they are scattered across a wall.

8. Cut the stems of your flowers so that the blooms just hang over the brim of the cones. Place a small bunch of flowers in each of the cones.

Hanging Easter Posies

Design: Justine Hand for Gardenista
Photography: Justine Hand for Gardenista

Materials:

- Ribbon
- Flowers
- Scissors
- Glue
- Some cleaned egg shells with the tops taken off (like a soft boiled egg)

How-To:

1. Measure a length of ribbon from the top of your window to the height you want your egg vases to hang. Double that measurement and cut your ribbon to that length. You can stagger the lengths slightly if you wish.

2. To attach the ribbon, brush or draw a thin line of glue starting at the opening of the egg, down one side, around the bottom, and up the opposite. Place the midpoint of your ribbon at the bottom center of the egg and press the ribbon into the line of glue.

3. To make sure that the ribbon adheres to the sides, cross the ends over the top of the egg and let them dry for several hours.

4. Arrange your flowers into a small bouquet. Measure the stems against your egg to make sure that the bouquet will fit in your vase.

5. Place the posy in the egg and water it.

6. Repeat with other arrangements.

7. Tie off the ends of your ribbons in a small bow and hang them with a tack in the window.

Carnation Garland

Styling: A Splendid Occasion
Floral Design: A Splendid Occasion
Photography: Karissa

Materials:

• Fishing line or thick embroidery thread

• Large needle

• 50 - 75 mini carnations (might be more or less depending on how long you want the garland to be)

• Scissors or floral shears

How-To:

1. Begin by cutting the stems off your carnations.

2. Thread the line or thread into the needle and secure the loose end by tying a simple loop knot.

3. Begin by pushing the needle through the front end of the flower (the pretty part) and it will come out of the back end (green side). Pull the wire through to the desired length and continue this step with all of the flowers.

4. Once you have all of the flowers threaded onto the string, tie a knot on both ends. Hang the garland above a beautiful cake or make a larger version for the background of your wedding ceremony. The options are endless!

Eggshell Flower Centerpiece

Crafting: Angie Ramirez
Photography: Angie Ramirez

This project is super fun to make and it looks fabulous as a centerpiece or side arrangement.

When you make breakfast, make sure to keep your egg shells by cracking the top of the egg carefully.

You can make one egg and place it on a single egg holder as a place setting or make a dozen and place them in a ceramic egg carton for a centerpiece.

Materials:

- 12 eggs
- Ceramic or cardboard egg carton
- Mixed bouquet of flowers
- Scissors
- Tweezers

How-To:

1. You will need to gather 12 eggs. Carefully crack each egg at the tip and open up a hole that is just large enough to allow the yolk to pass through. Wash out the eggshells.

2. Using some tweezers, remove the eggshell membranes as much as possible.

3. Wash out the eggs again, add water and place them in the carton.

4. Cut down the stems of your flowers to 3-4".

5. Arrange the flowers in the eggshells.

The Floral Frame

Crafting: Maggie Mao
Photography: Maggie Mao

It's always a pleasure to bring nature indoors. A touch of green will give any room a completely different look. This frame will look nice with any flowers you pick in your garden or in the park. Use scented flowers, hang the frame up by a window and enjoy the moments when the breeze brings the scent into the room.

Materials:

- Embroidery frame
- Test tube
- Monofilament fishing line
- Flowers of your choice
- Scissors

How-To:

1. Choose a test tube that will accommodate the stems of the flowers you want to use.

2. Cut a length of monofilament fishing line.

3. Lay the embroidery frame flat on a table or desk.

4. Position the test tube over the screw and secure by wrapping the line around the screw and test tube.

5. Tie a single or double knot in the fishing line and trim off any excess line.

6. Arrange the flowers in the tube and style however you'd like.

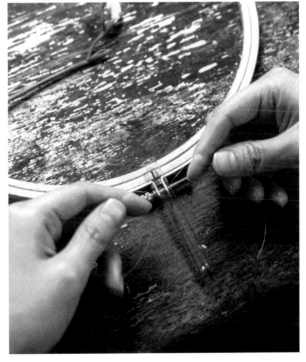

Dino Planters

Design: Dani Altamura
Crafting: Dani Altamura
Photography: Dani Altamura

Materials:

• Rubber dinosaur toys/figures

• Box cutter/X-acto knife

• Large sewing needle

• Spray paint

• Small plants (succulents as examples)

• Newspaper/drop sheet

• Painter's tape

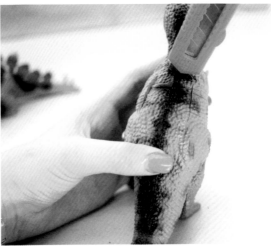

How-To:

1. First, decide which plant will go in which figure so you can determine the size of the holes you need to cut. The, carefully cut a hole in the back of each figure.

2. Next, use a large sewing needle to poke some drainage holes into the underside of each figure. Be careful! You can use your knife to cut some small holes/slits if the figure is too thick. Take note of the shape of the figure. If it slopes downward towards the tail, you may want to put the holes lower so that water doesn't pool inside the tail.

3. Give each figure a wash to remove any excess dust and dirt and let them dry completely.

4. Spread the figures out on the newspaper/drop sheet.

5. Give the spray paint a good shake and apply thin even coats to each figure. Be patient with this stage. Leave each coat so it's at least dry to the touch before applying the next coat. Your figures will have lots of small, awkward parts to reach, so you will need to do many coats from different angles before you have even coverage.

6. Let the paint dry overnight before adding a second color.

7. If you are adding a second color, tape off the areas you want to remain the first color. Again, it is important that your first color is completely dry at this stage or you will take the paint off with the tape!

8. Using the same method as before, add thin coats of the second color. Your color choice will determine how many coats you need to apply.

9. Once the paint is completely dry, you can remove the tape. If you have a sealer, you can apply a layer now.

10. Now you can pot your plants. This may be a little fiddly due to the size of the planters, but try to make sure that the soil if firmly packed. Otherwise, your plants are going to sink once you water them a couple of times.

11. Clean off any excess soil, water your plants and you're done! Place your new dino planters somewhere sunny and don't forget to water them.

Painted Air Plant Bell Cups

Concept: Chelsea Foy of Lovely Indeed
Crafting: Chelsea Foy of Lovely Indeed
Photography: Chelsea Foy of Lovely Indeed

Materials:

- Natural or bleached bell cups
- Craft paint in various shades
- Paintbrushes
- Painter's tape
- Tiny air plants

How-To:

1. Wipe down the bell cup with a dry cloth to rid it of any debris. If the bell cups are on sticks, you should be able to remove the stick from the bottom.

2. Place painter's tape around the bell cup about halfway down, in a horizontal stripe. Smooth the edges to be sure no paint seeps underneath. Paint the upper half of the bell cup.

3. Carefully remove the tape and set the cup aside for a few minutes to dry. Once dry, paint a complementary color around the top rim of the cup.

4. Once the cup is dry, pop your little air plant inside and set it on display!

Fresh Flower Cupcake Toppers

Crafting: Rachel Mae Smith
Photography: Rachel Mae Smith

Materials:

- Flowers

- Sponge

- Bamboo skewers

- Thin floral or jewelry wire

- Scissors

- Floral tape

How-To:

1. Cut your flowers short, leaving only about 1-1.5" of stem. You want enough to secure to the skewer, but you don't want the stem to go into the cupcake.

2. Cut a very thin layer of sponge and dip it in water. Aline your flower with the skewer (or slip it onto the skewer if you're able). Wrap the sponge around the skewer and base of the stem and tape it in place. You'll want to cover the tape with wire, or maybe even scrap fabric, so it does not show.

3. Place the toppers on your cupcakes and serve! If you are having several guests over, these would also look great on a larger cake. For reference, the ranunculus lasted 4 hours, the lilac 5 hours, and the daffodils 7.5 hours, all without refrigeration.

Fresh Flower Drink Stirrers

Floral Design/DIY: Pollen Floral Design
Photography: Cambria Grace Photography
Concept/Styling: Lauren Wells Events

Materials:

• Wood skewers

• Fresh flowers

• Gold embroidery thread

• Hot glue gun

How-To:

1. For larger flowers, such as a ranunculus or a poppy, snip off most of the stem, leaving a bit right under the flower head. For smaller flowers and wild flowers, such as chamomile or aster, use a stem with a small bunch of flowers on it.

2. For the larger flowers, you can simply skewer the stem. Piece of cake! For the smaller flowers, wrap the gold embroidery thread around the base of the stem to attach it to the skewer.

3. Place a dot of hot glue on the back of the embroidery thread, and use the glue to seal the thread.

4. Pour yourself a cocktail, and enjoy! The floral scent while you sip is just an added bonus.

Crystallized Flowers

Design: Tricia MacK
Crafting: Tricia MacK
Photography: Tricia MacK

These crystallized flowers taste as sweet
as they look. They are great as cake
toppers or as garnishes for desserts.

Kitchen brush

Egg white

Caster sugar

Nasturtium

How-To:

1. Wash the flowers thoroughly but gently, removing any dirt or insects. Lay them out to dry on a on tea towel.

2. Whisk the egg white until frothy. You may add a few drops of vodka to speed up the drying process.

3. Using a small kitchen brush, lightly coat the petals on both sides.

4. Using a teaspoon or your fingers, sprinkle caster sugar over the flower and shake to remove any excess. Repeat until each flower is coated with sugar.

5. Place the flowers on a wire rack lined with baking paper to dry for 24 hours.

6. Once completely dry, you can use these as cake toppers or store them in an airtight container for future use.

Flower Napkin Ring

Design: Tricia MacK
Crafting: Tricia MacK
Photography: Tricia MacK

Why use metal rings when you can wrap your napkins with nature's
beauty? This is a really simple project that lets flowers take center
stage in your table setting.

Materials:

• Your preferred flowers, preferably woody but not too brittle (crepe myrtle as an example)

• Kitchen string

How-To:

1. Wash and pat the flowers dry.

2. Cut the stems to 25-28 cm lengths and remove the leaves.

3. Bend the stems to form circles.

4. Secure the ends with string.

Bloom Gift Toppers

Creativity: Stephanie Brubaker
Design: Stephanie Brubaker
Photography: Stephanie Brubaker

Materials:

• Brown kraft boxes

• Washi tape

• Herbs

• Stems

• Branches and/or
blooms from your
yard, a nearby park or
your city block

When choosing your blooms, try to gather a variety of colors, shapes, textures, etc. And don't just go for the obvious choices. Throw some otherwise overlooked stems in there too for good measure. You may be surprised at the lovely combinations you come up with!

Foraged Gift Toppers

Creativity: Stephanie Brubaker
Design: Stephanie Brubaker
Photography: Stephanie Brubaker

Who needs expensive ribbon when you
have a few trees or bushes nearby? If you
start looking for little greens or twigs to
incorporate into your gifts, you will discover
so much overlooked beauty. It's really a
wonderful feeling!

Materials:

• Solid wrapping paper (brown kraft is a classic, but colors can also be lovely as they create contrast)

• Washi tape

• Twine

• Sprigs of greenery

Blooming Monograms

Design: Urbanic
Crafting: Urbanic
Photography: Urbanic

Materials:

• Paper mache letters
(there are 8" and 12")

• Box cutter

• Floral foam

• Glue gun

• Wire cutters or
strong scissors

• Silk flowers

How-To:

1. Using your box cutter, cut off the front of the letters and then hollow them out carefully.

2. Cut the foam into shapes that fit the letters and glue the foam into the hollows.

3. Trim the silk blooms off, leaving short stems. Push the stems into the foam and reinforce with glue if necessary.

4. Arrange the blooms however you'd like!

Lovely Air Plant Hanger

Design: Gloribell Lebron
Crafting: Gloribell Lebron
Photography: Gloribell Lebron

Valentine's Day doesn't have to be all pink and red. On this special celebration, try making something different and give love to your plants.

This craft is an accessory that can be given as a gift or you can make one (or several) to decorate your walls.

Materials:

• Galvanized steel chicken wire

• Air plants

• Metal snip pliers

• Spray paint (optional)

How-To:

1. Trace a heart shape on the wire.

2. Start by cutting around the heart shape. You may leave some pieces of wire that extend beyond the heart. After you're finished cutting, you can bend those pieces back, creating legs that will help the heart hang against the wall nicely.

3. Now, you can either spray paint the heart, or leave it its original color.

4. Arrange the air plants in the holes of the wire.

Air Plant and Moss Heart

Design: Gloribell Lebron
Crafting: Gloribell Lebron
Photography: Gloribell Lebron

Celebrate love with this beautiful heart made of air plants, moss,
and grapevines.

Materials:

- A grapevine heart
- Moss
- Air plants
- Glue gun

How-To:

1. Using a hot glue gun, start pasting pieces of moss onto the grapevine heart . Try mixing different types of moss to create visual interest.

2. To add vitality to the project, place some small air plants in the gaps between the moss. This heart can be hung with ribbon on a door or over a mantle.

Ombre Flora Heart

Blog Feature (project owner): The Knotty Bride
Project Creation: Kindred
Styling/Photography: Kindred

Materials:

- Heart papier mache box (comes with a lid, but you won't need it)

- Assorted fresh florals/greens

- Plastic wrap

- Floral foam for fresh flowers (make sure it is not "dry foam," which is used for fake flowers)

- Floral shears

How-To:

1. Line the inside of the box with plastic wrap. This will prevent water from soaking through when you add water to preserve the flowers.

2. Submerge the floral foam in water and let soak for about 15-20 minutes. Then, cut the foam to size to fit inside the heart.

3. Cut the stems of your flowers and greenery at a sharp angle with the floral shears. Use the pointed stems to puncture the foam and position your stems however you'd like. It may be necessary to create holes for the softer stems. Avoid doing this for the stems that are strong enough to be pushed into the foam because it doesn't allow the stems to take in as much water.

4. Now that your box is full of greens and pretty as ever, add an optional finishing touch by cutting out a message to lay on top!

Herb Wreath

Design: Tricia MacK
Crafting: Tricia MacK
Photography: Tricia MacK

This is a great way to use any overgrown herbs and bring the outside in. Hang it in the kitchen, so as the herbs dry, you will have easy access to them for cooking. This wreath looks pretty, smells absolutely delightful and makes a wonderful housewarming gift!

Materials:

• Your preferred herbs

• Embroidery hoop

• Kitchen string

• Scissors

How-To:

1. Make little bunches with each herb and tie them together with string.

2. Position the first bunch of herbs in the desired position on the hoop and secure with string.

3. Repeat with the other bunches of herbs, making sure the bunches overlap so as to cover the string.

Succulent Pumpkin

Design: Gloribell Lebron
Crafting: Gloribell Lebron
Photography: Gloribell Lebron

This project is fun to make and is definitely a different take on the
traditional Halloween pumpkin.

Materials:

- A grapevine pumpkin
- Some small succulents
- Glue gun
- Charcoal fiberglass screen
- Potting soil

How-To:

1. Remove the pumpkin stem so as to have access to the inside of the pumpkin.

2. Use a glue gun to attach the ribs that hold the vines together to the edge of the opening.

3. Gather the ends of the screen to form a pouch. Using a pencil, push the pouch inside the pumpkin. Fill the pouch with soil.

4. Begin by placing the largest succulents toward the top. Each succulent should have direct contact with the soil. Use the smaller succulents to fill in the gaps.

For the eyes, try using a different variety of succulent so that they stand out. For the mouth, using succulents with small leaves. To create a stem, try using Portulaca Molokiniensis Hobdy.

Book Planters for Succulents

Design: Russell Brown
Crafting: Russell Brown
Photography: Bethany Nauert

Materials:

• 1 Vintage book

• 2-3 small succulents (short and wide succulents work much better than tall ones)

• Potting soil

• Box cutter knife

• Parchment paper or plastic bag

• White glue

• Dry moss or ground cover

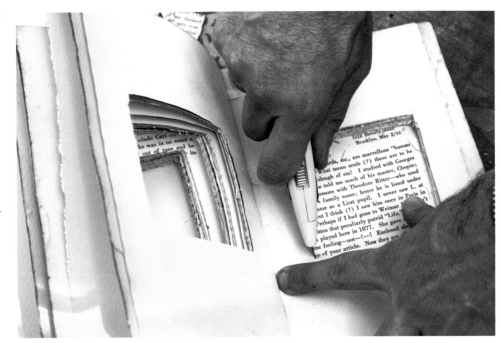

How-To:

1. The night before, rub a very thin layer of white glue against the paper edges so that some of the pages stick together. It doesn't need to be precise; it just helps when cutting into the book that the pages stay in one place.

2. Cutting the square in the book is the most time-consuming part. Decide how much space you want for planting. Start with the page after the title page and use your ruler to measure out a square or rectangle to suit your needs. Cut through a few pages at a time, pull them out, and work your way down the book. You will need a hole that is at least 1 1/2 inches deep. The hole does not need to be clean or pretty because the only page that will be visible is the top page, so don't worry if the other pages tear badly, or look jagged. By the time the rest of the hole is made, you will have a better sense of how to make the cutout for the title page centered and clean. Remember this is the only page where the look of the cutout matters.

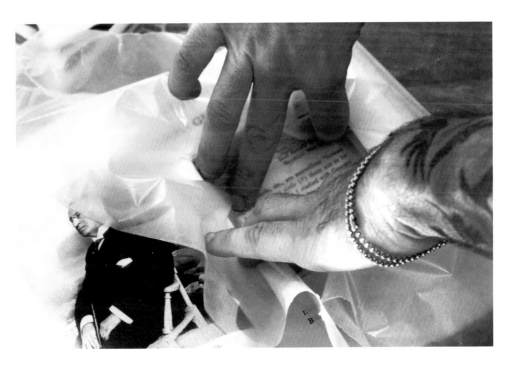

3. Line the hole with parchment paper or plastic. This just prevents any watering from damaging the rest of the book.

4. If your book is very, very deep, you can put a layer of gravel at the bottom of the hole. This will provide some drainage that your succulents will appreciate. In an average sized book you won't have room for gravel.

5. Start with the main succulent and separate it from the soil it's packed in. Place it in the hole where you like. Repack the soil around it so it can stand on its own. For the larger plants, you will need to wedge them into the corners so they stand up until they start to grow on their own. You will need to pack the soil tightly around the roots to make them stand. A little water in the soil will also help.

6. Once you have the succulents where you want, cover the soil in dry moss. Or you can leave the soil exposed if you like.

7. Cut the parchment paper just below the surface of the moss so that its adequately hidden.

Note: About once a week, spray a little bit of water into the roots with a squirt bottle. If you are keeping them inside, make sure they are by a window or put them outside as much as possible. When you water them, try to avoid getting water on the title page.

Paper Succulent

Design: Lucy Akins
Crafting: Lucy Akins
Photography: Lucy Akins

These look fairly lifelike in photos, but they look even better in person.

These succulents are easy to make and you can place them in a frame or wreath without having to worry about making a mess or watering.

Materials:

- Thick cardstock (Canvas Corp Handmade Thickstock as example)

- DecoArt Americana acrylic paint in Hauser Medium Green

- DecoArt Americana acrylic paint in Antique Green

- DecoArt Americana acrylic paint in White

- Scissors

- Hot glue gun

How-To:

1. Mix the white paint with the greens to make various shades.

2. Apply paint to both sides of the paper, making sure the various shades of greens are visible. Allow the paper to dry.

3. Draw and cut out various sizes of petals as shown in the pictures.

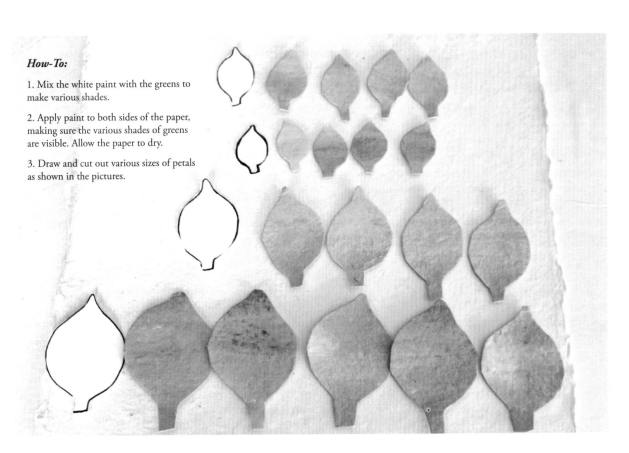

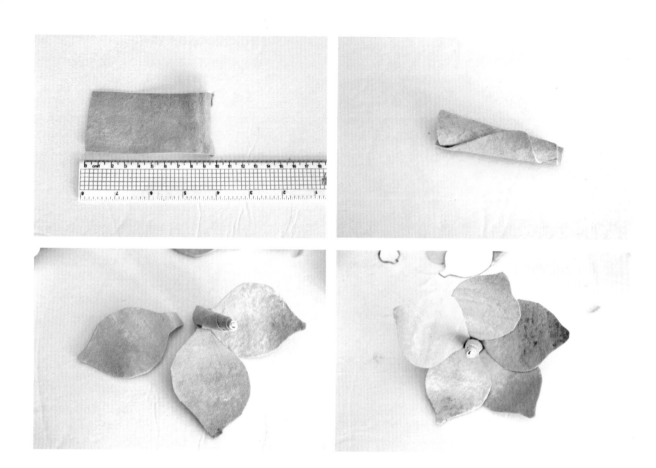

4. Cut a rectangle that is approximately 10 cm long out of the paper and roll it as shown above to create the center and stem of your succulent. Secure the larger end with hot glue.

5. Glue larger petals to the stem, starting at the bottom.

6. As you work up the stem, decrease the size of your petals. Make sure you leave space in between each layer of petals, so the stem is visible.

7. Once you are done gluing, you can paint on some additional shading. To make your succulent look even more realistic, you can add a light outline of purple to the petals.

Note: Study photos of real succulents and play
around with shading and purple tones.

Crepe Paper Flowers

Design: Marilyn and Kaleb Nimz
Crafting: Marilyn and Kaleb Nimz
Photography: Marilyn and Kaleb Nimz

Materials:

• Green and pink crepe paper streamers

• Wooden skewers

• Gold tinsel garland

• Glue gun with glue sticks

• Scissors

How-To:

1. Cut two strips of green crepe paper about 5" long. Cut about 20 small strips of pink crepe paper about 3" long. An easy way to cut several of the pink strips at a time is to roll it around something 3" wide and then cut the ends.

2. Cut the strips of pink crepe paper into ovals by rounding the corners. You want to maintain both the width and length. You can cut several at once if you stack the strips on top of each other squarely and use sharp scissors to cut. When you are finished with this, stretch out the center of your ovals gently with your thumbs. Leave the edges of the ovals unstretched. Stack two petals together and crease them about 1/2'' up from the bottom. Repeat with all leftover petals. Once this is complete, you can use your glue gun to glue your petals to each other. Layer the petals so that they overlap to create a tulip shape.

3. Use hot glue to adhere a wooden skewer to the bottom part of your tulip. Hold in place until the glue is dry. Carefully dot a length of green crepe paper with glue and wrap it tightly around the skewer, starting at the top. Once you reach the bottom, continue wrapping back up the skewer again to end in the middle. Glue the end in place.

4. Trim the 5'' pieces of green crepe paper from step 1 into leaf shapes. Glue them onto the skewer. Once they are secured, you can stretch out the centers go to give them some shape.

5. Use your scissors to trim your gold tinsel garland into 2" strips. Crease the strips about a centimeter from the bottom. Take one piece of tinsel, dot the folded part with glue and secure to the inside of your tulip. Repeat with the other tinsel pieces. Be careful with the glue as it can melt the tinsel.

Crepe Peony

Design: Lucy Akins
Crafting: Lucy Akins
Photography: Lucy Akins

Materials:

• White crepe paper

• Yellow and red food coloring

• Microwave safe plate

• Scissors

• Floral wire

• Floral tape

• Hot glue gun or quick drying glue

• Yellow embroidery thread

• Double sided tape

• A large dish with 1/4" of water in it

How-To:

1. Add food coloring to the dish of water. You can use three drops of red and two drops of yellow for the outer petals and three drops of yellow and one drop of red for the inner petals. Experiment with the amount of food coloring to achieve the look you want.

2. Cut a 4"x 4" square of crepe paper through the folded layers and dip into the food coloring mixture. Make sure that the color penetrates through all the layers.

3. Allow the paper to drip dry for a couple of minutes. You can simply hang the paper off the side of the bowl.

4. Place the paper on a microwave safe dish and heat for 30-40 seconds at a time (time for drying will vary according to thickness of paper and make of microwave). Please make sure you monitor the drying process and do not exceed more than 40 seconds at a time. The paper will burn in the center if left in the microwave for too long.

5. Once the paper is dry, cut several petals at once. Make sure the grain runs with height.

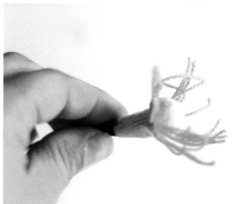

6. Sculpt the petals with a cupping technique. You do this by holding either side of a petal with your thumbs and forefingers. Slowly stretch the entire width of the petal with both hands, using the thumbs to push into and cup the petal and the forefingers to stretch the paper away from the thumbs.

7. To make the stamen, wrap the embroidery thread around your middle and index fingers approximately 9 times.

8. Slip the thread off your fingers and cut at the top and bottom of the loop.

9. Tape the thread onto double sided tape as shown; set aside.

10. Form a ball from a scrap of crepe paper. Encase the ball in a larger piece of crepe paper as shown above.

11. Insert floral wire into the center and tape down the edges with floral tape.

12. Take the double sided tape and thread and tape around stamen.

13. Using a glue gun or quick drying glue, start gluing petals around the stamen.

14. Continue gluing petals on until the desired size is achieved.

Paper Coffee Filter Flowers

Design: SoulMakes
Crafting: SoulMakes
Photography: SoulMakes

Materials:

- White basket coffee filters
- Acrylic paint
- Bowls
- Water
- Scissors
- Wire
- Newspaper
- Floral tape

How-To:

1. Fill some large plastic bowls with water to the halfway point. Add a glop of acrylic paint and stir. Drop a handful of filters into each color, ring them out and set them aside to dry overnight.

2. Once the filters are dry, fold them into fourths.

3. Cut petal shapes out of the wide fan part of your filters.

4. Cut a variety of sizes. You'll want at least two of each size. You can go as big or as small as you want.

5. Unfold the filters and lay them on top of each other from largest to smallest.

6. Cut about a foot of wire. Make a knot at one end of your wire and stick the other end through the middle of all your filters. The knotted end will keep the wire from slipping all the way through the paper.

7. Starting with your smallest cut out, begin peeling up and folding each layer of paper one by one.

8. Fluff as needed.

9. Pinch the bottom of the flower to create a good shape.

10. Wrap the wire around the base a few times to hold it all together.

If you want to, you can make a stem for these beauties very easily.

1. Tear off a small piece of newspaper.

2. Roll it up to create a thin stem.

3. Using the excess wire hanging out of your flower, attach the rolled paper onto the pinched base of your flower. Twist the paper a bit and continue wrapping the wire all the way down.

4. Starting at the tope, wrap floral tape down the length of your stem.

Note: If you don't attach a stem, you can use the excess wire to wrap your flowers around all sorts of things around your house (e.g. a bed post, a stair rail, a chair back, shutters, etc.)

Realistic Paper Roses

Design: Hannah Hathaway
Crafting: Hannah Hathaway
Photography: Hannah Hathaway

Materials:

- White crepe paper

- Microwaveable bowl and plate

- Paint brush

- Acrylic paint section on its own bullet point

- Clean spray bottle filled with water.

- Microwave

- Hot glue gun

How-To:

1. Cut your petals out. To make your flowers look super realistic, cut the petals with the vein of the paper flowing vertically.

2. With your bowl facing upside down on your plate, lightly spray the bowl's surface with water and place your petals on the bowl. Now you can start painting. If you are using a strong color, you may want to water down your paint. In this example, pink and yellow were used to create a coral.

3. Once all your petals are painted, spray them with water to let the colors blend together. The more you spray, the lighter the color will turn out. If you want the color to bleed through to the other side, make sure to give them a good soaking.

4. To dry your petals, microwave on high for 30 seconds at a time until dry. It may take as long as 3 minutes in total.

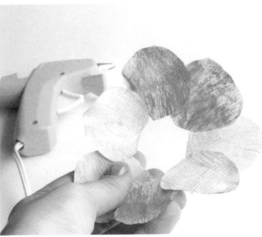

5. When they are dry, the petals will peel off in a lovely concave shape. You can give the petals the lovely natural creases and ripples real petals have by pressing them into the palm of your hand.

6. To make a large rose, you need to start out with a large ring of petals. Glue petals together until you have a nice curvy circle. You want the rings to bend in toward the center, almost like a cup.

7. Make 5 or 6 rings of petals, each one slightly smaller than the last, with the petals overlapping more and more.

8. Add some curled up center petals and stack and glue all your rings of petals together to make one lovely rose.

Cake Pop Rosebuds

Design: Cakegirls
Crafting: Cakegirls
Photography: Cakegirls

Show your sweetie how much you care with
these fancy little cake pop rosebuds. Filled
with a delicious surprise inside, these look
like the real thing and smell just as sweet.

Materials:

- 16 oz. store-bought pound cake
- 1 tub store-bought icing
- 8 oz. Fondarific Hot Pink rolled fondant icing
- 8 oz. Fondarific Red rolled fondant icing
- 16 oz. white candy coating
- JEM Easy Rose Petal Cutter 110mm
- Set of 50 6" x 5/32" sucker sticks
- 2 grams luster dust in Tulip Red
- Paintbrushes
- Fat Daddio's 1 3/8" stainless steel scoop or tablespoon
- Food processor
- Tray or cookie sheet

How-To:

1. Cut the cake into chunks and then pulse them in the bowl of a food processor until crumbly and coarse.

2. Add about 1/3 of a tub of frosting to the crumbs. Pulse a few more times to mix, but do not over puree. The mixture should hold together when squeezed.

3. Using a scoop or a tablespoon, scoop out 1 level tablespoon of filling.

4. Roll into a teardrop shape with your hands. Continue with the rest of the filling and place the teardrops on a tray. Refrigerate for 1/2 hour or until very firm before adding the sticks.

5. Place some white candy coating in the microwave on half power and heat in 30 second intervals, stirring in between until melted.

6. Remove one teardrop from the fridge. Using a sucker stick, poke a hole in the rounded end of the teardrop. Push the stick half way up the teardrop, remove the stick, dip in melted coating and reinsert into the teardrop. Swipe away any dripping coating. Place back in the fridge and then continue, one-by-one, with each remaining teardrop.

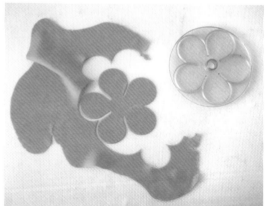

7. On a surface covered lightly with powdered sugar, roll out a small portion of hot pink fondant as thinly as possible.

8. Use the rose cutter to cut out a flower shape.

9. Place the fondant flower in your palm with the center resting at an opening between your fingers. Brush the middle of the flower with a very light coating of water and push a sucker stick (already attached to a teardrop) through the center of the fondant.

10. Referring to the numbers on the rose cutter, lift and stretch petal no. 1 up and around the teardrop. Repeat the process with petal no. 2, making sure it cups and attaches to petal no. 1 to cover the teardrop cake pop. Brush with a little water to help the petals adhere as necessary.

11. Repeat the process again with petal no. 3, no. 4 and no. 5. Make sure to place these petals evenly around the outside of the bud.

12. Use water to help the petal adhere as needed.

13. Once the petals are in place, use your fingers to curl and flair the edges of the petals for effect.

14. Using a dry paintbrush, heavily dab the inside and edges of the rosebud with Tulip Red luster dust. Gently turn the cake pop upside down and brush off the excess onto a piece of wax paper or parchment paper. Recoat in layers as desired.

Clay Flower Magnets

Design: Tricia MacK
Crafting: Tricia MacK
Photography: Tricia MacK

Create delicate flowers with clay and add
magnets to adorn your fridge with.

Materials:

• Fimo clay (or other
modeling clay, if you prefer)

• Ceramic magnets

• Skewer

• Hot glue gun

• Pearl/beads (optional)

For camellia:

1. Roll 10-15 balls of clay and flatten into thin oval pieces of varying sizes.

2. Roll one piece of clay into the camellia bud, by rounding, scrunching and pressing in gently.

3. Add petals around the bud, using bigger pieces of clay for the outer layers of the camellia.

For four petal flower:

1. Roll 5 equal sized balls of clay and flatten each one to make a circle of ~ 2 cm.

2. The first circle will be your flower base. With the remaining circles, use your thumb and index finger to pinch into petals.

3. Attach petals onto the base and press to secure with blunt end of skewer.

4. Pinch the rounded end of each petal.

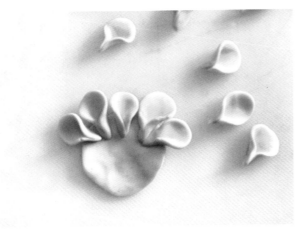

For chrysanthemum:

1. Roll and flatten one ball of clay to form ~2 cm base.

2. Roll 20-25 smaller balls of clay to form ~ 1 cm circles when flattened.

3. Pinch the smaller circles with your thumb and index finger to form little petals.

4. Attach around the circumference of the base.

5. Keep adding petals, making sure to overlap to cover gaps.

Once you have made the flowers, pop them on a baking paper in a baking tray to bake in the oven for 30 minutes at 110 degrees Celsius.

Once baked, allow to cool to room temperature so the clay completely hardens.

Add pearls/beads to centre of flowers if you like, using a hot glue gun.

Hot glue the ceramic magnets to the base of each flower.

Fabric Flowers

Design: Lexy Ward of The Proper Pinwheel
Styling: Lexy Ward of The Proper Pinwheel
Photography: Lexy Ward of The Proper Pinwheel

These DIY fabric flowers are the perfect gift to
give to someone special. Whether in a bouquet
or formed as a brooch, the flowers will last far
longer than a few days!

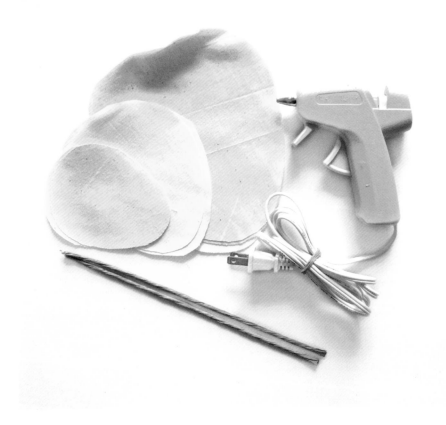

Materials:

• Assorted fabric cut into egg-like shapes in three different sizes

• Floral stem wire

• Hot glue gun

How-To:

1. Starting with the smallest fabric petal, place a small dollop of hot glue in the bottom left hand side. Fold the petal half lengthwise and press to secure.

2. Once folded, lay the petal flat and place another dollop of hot glue at the bottom. Grab the top layer of the petal and keep the raw edges aligned, press it into the glue to form a cone shape.

3. Repeat this process with all of your petals.

4. Working one petal at a time, hot glue them onto the stem. To do so, place a small amount of glue inside the petal on top of the glued folds. Press the folded area around the stem as shown.

5. Once glued, the petal will be leaning forward. Fold the petal back to open it up.

6. Rotate the stem a bit, and glue on another small petal using the same technique.

7. Glue on the rest of your petals using the same technique, working from smallest to largest until complete.

Feel free to add in fabrics with varying textures like burlap and tulle. They add dimension and really complement the aesthetic.

To make a brooch, follow the instructions for making the petals. Instead of attaching them to the stem, glue the folded areas together using the same rotation and shaping techniques.

Corn Husk Flower Garland

Design: Sharon Garofalow for YouAreMyFave.com
Crafting: Sharon Garofalow for YouAreMyFave.com
Photography: Sharon Garofalow for YouAreMyFave.com

Here is a really easy DIY for making corn husk flowers that
will be the perfect addition to your holiday decorations.

Materials:

- Corn husks

- Scissors

- Scrap paper (one piece of scrap for each flower you make)

- Glue gun

- Curling iron

How-To:

1. Separate the corn husks. They will be stuck together in the package, but will pull apart really easily. Cut out a petal shape from a corn husk. These do not have to be perfect, so you can freehand them. You will need 3 graduated sizes for each petal and there are 5 petals to each flower.

2. Simply hot glue one set of the three sizes together at the bottom of each petal. Continue with all 5 sets.

3. Go plug in your curling iron. Curl the ends of each petal to your liking. Much like hair, the larger the barrel, the larger the curl. Once they are all curled, lay out the petals so you can see how you'd like to arrange your flower.

4. Glue the petals to a small piece of scrap paper. They should overlap and be spaced relatively evenly.

5. It is super easy to make different size flowers and you can easily make them into a garland with a little tape on the back. Tape won't stick to the corn husk, but will to the paper.

Fabric Flowers

Design: Michelle Edgemont
Crafting: Michelle Edgemont
Photography: Michelle Edgemont

Using fabric and branches, this project will
create everlasting flowers to gift to a loved one
on a special occasion or to decorate a room with.
Gather the branches from your yard or local
park. You can use any color of fabric you wish.

Materials:

- 1/4 yard each of four sheer fabrics in different colors
- Scissors
- Card stock
- Pencil
- Quilting ruler
- Rotary cutter
- Cutting mat
- Hot glue gun
- Found branches
- Thread
- Needle

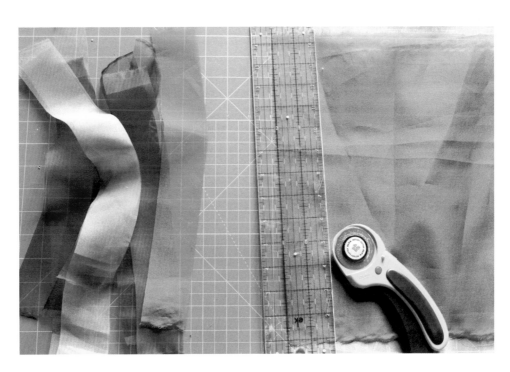

How-To:

1. Fold the tulle fabric in half and lay flat on the cutting mat.

2. Using the quilting ruler and rotary cutter, cut two 2" strips for the petals of each flower and one 1" strip for the center of each flower.

3. Cut the card stock into a 2" x 2" piece. Draw a design for your petals on this piece of card stock. Refer to the photo for options of petal designs.

4. Cut out the petal design from the card stock.

5. Take one 2" strip and wrap it around the card stock stencil.

6. While holding the stencil and the fabric, follow the stencil with your scissors cutting the petals out of the fabric.

7. Unfold the fabric strip.

8. Use your needle and thread to make long running stitches all along the bottom of the fabric strip.

9. Cut the thread at the end. Push the fabric toward the knot, creating a circle. Stitch the ends of the circle of petals together.

10. Repeat steps 5-9 with the second 2" strip of fabric.

11. Fold the 1" strip of fabric over on itself until it is about 1/2" wide. Use your scissors to cut strips in the top half to create a fringe.

12. Unfold the strip and sew wide running stitches along the bottom of the fabric strip. Push the fabric toward the knot and sew the ends together.

13. Push the branch through the center of your fringe piece. Secure the fringe piece to the top of the branch with glue. Glue the two petal circles around the center fringe.

14. Repeat the above steps to create as many flowers as you'd like to make.

Paper Spider Mums

Design: Kelly S. Rowe
Crafting: Kelly S. Rowe
Photography: Kelly S. Rowe

Materials:

- 12"×12" card stock paper, in colors of choice
- Fringe scissors or large cutting scissors
- Tape
- Floral wire stems
- Green floral tape
- Glue or hot glue gun

How-To:

1. Cut your paper into 2-3" wide strips. You can play with the sizes to best fit what you're looking for. Once your strips are cut, take your fringe scissors or a large pair of scissors and cut fringe into the tops of your strips.

2. Roll the strips of paper up to form your bud. You can place some double-sided tape inside while you roll it to help secure it, if you'd like.

3. Once you're done rolling up your bud, tape it closed.

4. Glue your floral wire stem to the center of your bud (at the bottom).

5. Now it's time to wrap the bud and stem together. Because the diameter of the bud is larger than that of the stem, you'll want to use some tissue paper or something similar to help create a taper from the bud to the stem. Wrap your floral tape around the bud, over your tissue, and down the stem.

6. Once you've completely wrapped (and merged) the bud and stem together, you're done assembling.

7. Finish your flower by fanning out the paper strips. Use your thumb to give a gentle curve to each strip.

A Gorgeous Lotus Bud

Design: Eleanna Kotsikou
Crafting: Eleanna Kotsikou
Photography: Eleanna Kotsikou

Materials:

• 6" x 6" squares of colorful origami paper

• Paper craft glue or hot glue gun

• Wooden skewers

• Scissors

• Paper clips

• Pen

• Objects: one with a diameter of 5.5" and another with a diameter of 2.6"

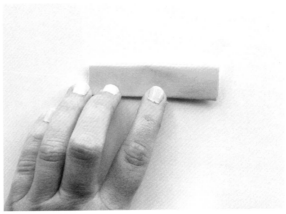

How-To:

1. To make the stamen, you will need a strip of paper, so cut a 6" x 6" square in half. Fold the strip of paper in half to form a square. With the fold at the top, fold the square in half again by bringing the top down to the bottom. Fold the paper in half again by bringing the folded top down to the bottom. This will create a slim strip. Fold the strip in half width-wise.

2. Take a pair of scissors and holding the paper along the fold, cut small vertical cuts into the top. This will create a paper fringe. At this point, cut open the side folds to allow the "stamen" to open up a bit more.

3. Unfold your stamen and make a small hole in the center along the fold. Insert a wooden skewer through the hole. Apply some glue to the top side of the paper below the fringe. Fold the sides back together around the skewer and hold in place until the glue has dried. When dry, gently separate the individual strips of paper to give the stamen more volume and a natural, fluffy shape.

 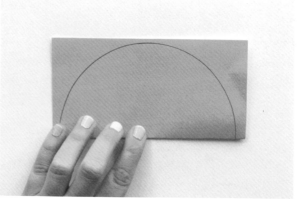

4. To create the lotus bud, use paper that is a different color from your stamen. Place the paper colored side up on your work surface. Place a circular object like a bowl with a 5.5" diameter on top of the paper and trace.

5. Turn the paper over. Bring the bottom edge up to meet the top edge, and fold in half horizontally. Crease well. Open up the paper again and take the left edge over to meet the right edge, and fold in half vertically, as pictured below. Crease well. Bring the bottom left corner up to the top right-corner, and fold the paper diagonally. You should have a triangle, as pictured below. Unfold the paper and fold it again on the other diagonal, so that the lower right corner meets the upper left corner. Crease well.

6. Unfold the paper and place a circular object like a jam jar lid with a diameter of around 2.6" in the center of the white side of the paper and trace around it.

7. Carefully cut out the bigger circle. Make sure to cut inside the pen marks so that they are removed. Place the circle on a flat and soft object like an eraser or a piece of clay. Use the sharp end of the skewer to create a small hole in the center of the circle. Now cut along the eight lines created by the folds until you reach the smaller circle. If it helps, trace the folds with a pen first, so that you can see them clearly.

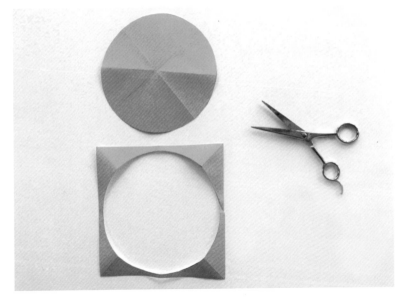

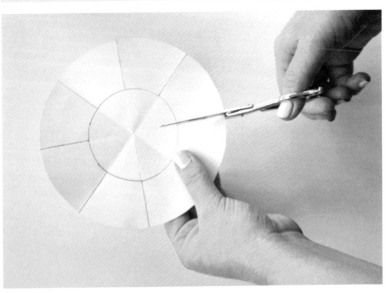

8. Place the paper on a flat surface with the colored side facing down. Fold every other petal toward the center. Dot glue on the left-hand corner of each folded petal. Glue each petal to the next folded one. Overlap the petals in the same direction. Make sure to glue them fairly closely so that you leave space for the second layer of petals. But also ensure that you've left enough room for the stamen to pass through the central hole.

9. Now, add a bit of glue on the upper right corner of the remaining petals. Glue each petal to the one on its right to form the second layer of the bulb. You may find it useful to keep the petals in place with a paper clip until they dry. Insert the stem with the stamen through the hole, glue it in place and your lotus bulbs are ready.

Paper Lilies

Design: Eleanna Kotsikou
Crafting: Eleanna Kotsikou
Photography: Eleanna Kotsikou

Materials:

• 6" x 6" squares of colorful origami paper

• Paper craft glue or hot glue gun

• Waxed thread

• Wooden skewers

• Scissors

How-To:

1. Start with three pieces of paper that are the same color. Place one square of paper on a flat surface with the colored side facing down. Fold the paper in two by bringing the lower edge up to the top, leaving a space of about 0.2'' as pictured above. Crease well. Use a bone folder or the back of a metal spoon for perfectly sharp folds. Starting from one of the short sides, fold or pleat the paper accordion-style, making each pleat about a centimeter wide. Each time you fold, crease well. When done, unfold the paper.

2. Repeat the process with the two other sheets of paper. Make sure the white strips at the top and the pleats are the same width on all three pieces. Precision is key here.

3. Glue the three separate pieces of folded paper together, one next to the other, to create a long strip of accordion paper. To do so, add some paper craft glue on the edge of one end and overlap with the next piece of paper. You'll need to hold the pieces together until the glue has set. Stand the long accordion strip up, so that it forms a tube. Glue the last two ends together to close the circle. Now, the accordion tube that will form the petals is ready!

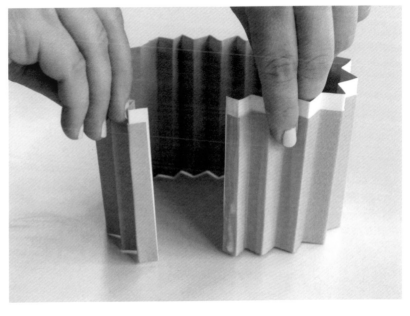

4. Cut two 16" length of thread. Try to use thread in a contrasting color to the paper you've used for the petals. Fold the two pieces of thread in half and wrap them around the wooden skewer. Glue the thread about 5 cm from the top of the skewer, and knot securely. Tie knots toward the ends of the threads. Vary where you tie the knot on each thread. Trim off the excess.

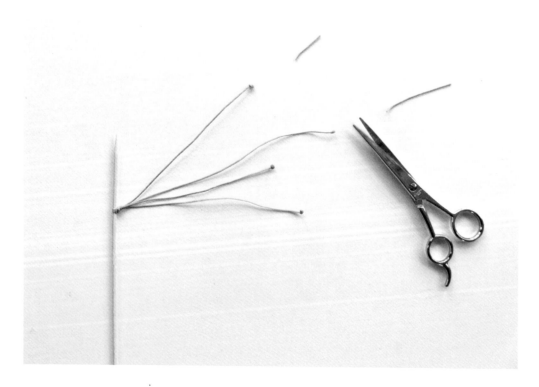

5. Now you are set to glue the petals on the stem. If you have a hot glue gun, use it to complete this step. Follow the instructions regardless of the type of glue you are using. Dot the inside bottom edge of the accordion tube with glue. Insert the bottom of the skewer through the top of the tube so that the stamen threads hang out the top of the tube as pictured.

Press the bottom half of the petals together. You need to ensure that the glue sticks to the inner side of each fold, and that the paper tube sticks to the skewer. Make sure the stick stays in the center of the folds.

If you didn't use a glue gun, you might need to use some paper clips to hold the petals together. Leave the flower to dry upside-down.

Once the glue has dried, your pretty paper lily is ready to be used. You can make a smaller lily using just two sheets of paper.

Paper Flowers

Design: Claire Cassidy
Crafting: Claire Cassidy
Photography: Claire Cassidy

Materials:

- Sheets of 8.5" x 11" brown paper
- Sheets of 8.5" x 11" white paper
- Small pieces of neon paper
- Wooden sticks
- Transparent tape
- Black washi tape
- Pencil
- Scissors
- Tweezers

How-To:

1. To make the center of the flower, cut two squares of white paper. Less than a quarter of a sheet will do. Scrunch up one square into a ball and cover with the second square. Place this on top of the wooden stick, secure with transparent tape. Be sure to wrap the tape tightly and tape all the way down to the stick, otherwise the paper will slide off.

2. Cut your neon paper into five or six small strips. Use transparent tape to fix these one by one around the bud. The tweezers will help you slot each piece in as you wrap the tape around. You can add one more layer of tape at this point, just to keep everything secure.

3. Now you are ready to make the petals. Each flower uses twelve petals. To create twelve, stack two sheets of brown paper together and fold them in half lengthwise. Mark off three even sections on the paper and draw a petal shape in each section. They should be balloon-shaped. It is easier to fix them to the stick with the little tail on the end. Hold all four layers together and cut through all of your pencil lines. Cut slightly inside the lines so that you don't end up with any visible pencil marks. You'll now have twelve petals. Scrunch each petal into a ball.

4. To fix the petals to the stick, uncurl them and wrap the tail end around the stick just under the bud. Attach each petal one at a time with transparent tape. Rotate the flower after each petal placement to ensure the petals are even spread around the bud. At this point all of the petals will be facing upward, and the flower will look a little closed – you will curl them out later.

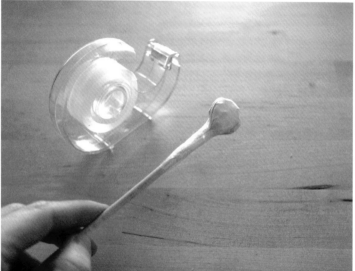

5. Once you have all your petals added, use the black washi tape to cover the transparent tape. Wind it tightly, and continue down until you reach the stick. Next, you can shape the flower. Starting from the outermost petals, gently bend each one back against your finger until it curves outwards. The crumple of the paper should help the petals take shape easily.

6. Pop them in a vase or jar, and you are done!

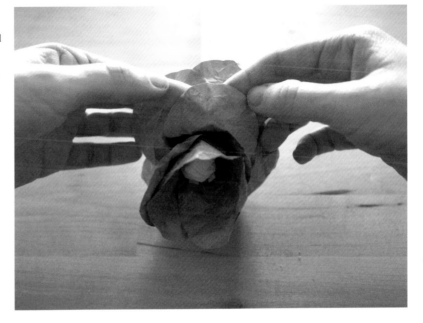

Book Page Flower Ring

Design: Fanfan Yang
Crafting: Fanfan Yang
Photography: Fanfan Yang

Materials:

• Old book pages

• Scissors

• Ring blank

• Small jewel

• Flower shape stencil that is 2.5" to 3" in diameter

• PVA glue

How-To:

1. Use the stencil to cut 4 of flower shapes out of the old book pages.

2. Cut one petal shape out of the first flower, then two out of the second, three out of the third, and four out of the fourth, as shown. Discard the pieces you cut out.

3. Take one flower shape and glue the petals on either side of the cutout together. This will create a cone shape. Repeat this process with each flower.

4. Curl the petals to create a softer shape. Next, put your finger in the middle of the biggest flower and press down. Glue it to the ring blank. Cut off the pointed bottoms of the rest of the flowers.

5. Dot glue in the center of the biggest flower and place the rest of the flowers inside, starting with the largest and ending with the smallest.

6. Glue the small jewel in the center.

Recycled Seeded Paper Flowers

Creativity: Sharon Langsdale - Razzle Dazzle Rose
Design: Sharon Langsdale - Razzle Dazzle Rose

Materials:

• Die cut paper flower kits

• Scissors

• Glue

• Pin

How-To:

1. Buy the die cut paper flower kits from your local eco craft materials shop. You can choose from recycled brown kraft paper flowers, cream vintage fleck flowers, or seeded paper flowers. This example uses the cream vintage fleck flower kit from Razzle Dazzle Rose.

2. To make the flower, you need to carefully roll the paper from the outer end until you reach the middle.

3. Once you are finished rolling the flower, you'll need to add some glue to the large area in the center. Press the rolled flower into the glue. Once you let go of the rolled flower, it will unroll slightly. This is OK as you'll want the flower petals to look a bit looser and more natural.

Sharon finds that lifting the rolled flower in one hand and squeezing a blob of glue under the rolled part works best. You then need to add another blob of glue to the rest of the middle part, and squeeze the flower together.

4. Leave the glue to set for 20 minutes; then start to bend the petals away from the center. By moving and bending the petals, you create a more natural look for your petals.

5. You can create fantastic button holes by gluing a pin to the back.

Christmas Paper Flower

Creativity: Lucy Akins
Design: Lucy Akins
Photography: Lucy Akins

Materials:

- Patterned thick card stock

- Scissors

- Glue

- Hot Glue

- Gold glitter (optional)

How-To:

1. Download the templates here and print:
http://www.craftberrybush.com/2013/11/
christmas-paper-flower-tutorial.html

Or create your own templates. You'll need two flowers with a 4.5" diameter, 2 with a 3.5" diameter, and another 2 with a 2" diameter. Each flower should have 5 petals. You'll also need two branches that are 5.5" long, and one that is 4.5" long. You can freehand the leaves however you'd like.

2. Cut the flowers and branches out of the patterned card stock.

3. Add glitter to branches.

4. Wrap the petals around a pencil so that they curl in.

5. Glue the flowers together by placing a small amount of glue in the center of each flower. Work from largest to smallest.

6. Add glitter to the center of the flower if desired.

7. Hot glue the flower and branches onto a gift.

Paper Poppies

Design: Lia Griffith
Crafting: Lia Griffith
Photography: Lia Griffith

This orange paper poppy is easy to make. You can wear it in your hair or put it on top of a gift to add a special touch. Once you have your print, just follow the step-by-step tutorial to create this cheerful bloom.

Materials:

• Paper poppy PDF

• Printed front and back on text weight paper

• Scissors

• Hot glue gun

• Mini clothespin (optional)

How-To:

1. Download the paper poppy PDF here: http://liagriffith.com/make-some-paper-poppies/

2. Print side one, then turn the paper over and print side two.

3. Trim all the pieces.

4. Cut a fringe into the edges of the circular pieces.

5. Curl the fringe to make cup shapes.

6. Fold the seven petals like paper fans (see image on previous page).

7. Cut the tops of the petals with the edge of your scissors so they will fan away from the center of the flower once it is assembled. Cut two slits at the bottom of each petal.

8. Overlap the two strips of paper at the bottom of each petal and glue them together so that each petal forms a cup shape.

9. Glue the overlapped bottoms of three light petals together to form a round layer of petals. Do the same with four dark petals.

10. Stack the three petal layer inside the four petal layer and secure with glue.

11. Glue the pink fringe into the center.

12. Glue the black fringe into the center.

13. Glue the green piece to the bottom of the poppy. Glue the pin to the bottom.

14. Your poppy is finished!

Mini Tissue Poms and Flower Gift Toppers

Design: Lia Griffith
Crafting: Lia Griffith
Photography: Lia Griffith

These mini tissue poms and flower gift toppers are just too cute! They are a perfect decoration for baby showers, bridal showers, princess parties, and even Mother's Day.

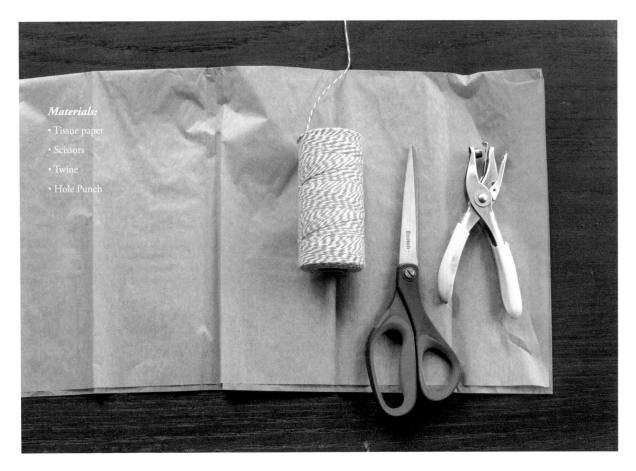

How-To:

1. Fold a large square of tissue in half twice. At this point you should have four layers.

2. Fold again for 8 layers.

3. And once again for 16 layers.

4. Fold diagonally to create a triangle.

5. Fold the triangle in half to form a smaller triangle.

6. Fold half of the triangle again and turn over. See images on the next page.

7. Fold the other half of the triangle to form a small triangle.

8. Draw a half circle onto the triangle to form a teardrop shape with the folded corner as the point.

9. Trim the tissue along the half circle with scissors, discarding the top part of the triangle.

10. Open the tissue petals and stack eight layers, rotating as you go.

11. If you are making a flower, skip the next step.

12. If you are making a pom, continue stacking the last eight layers, rotating as you go.

13. Fold the petal stack in half and punch a hole in the center, when you reopen the petals, you will have two holes.

14. Tie twine through hole.

15. Flatten the petals again and starting with the top layer, gather the tissue into a cone and crimp at the base. Complete eight layers for pom and all layers for the flower.

16. For the pom, turn to the other side and fluff and crimp the last eight layers toward the opposite direction.

17. Tie these on top of gifts or use them for party decorations.

Cocktail Napkin Flower Garland

Design: Lia Griffith
Crafting: Lia Griffith
Photography: Lia Griffith

These simple tissue flowers can be attached to ribbon to create a garland that makes a gorgeous backdrop. It can be used for bridal showers, baby showers or a photo backdrop for a dreamy event. Of course you can use any color of cocktail napkin to make your garland.

206

Materials:

- Cocktail napkins
- Scissors
- Round reinforcement labels
- Ribbon
- Ruler

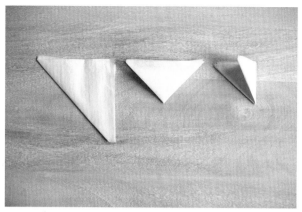 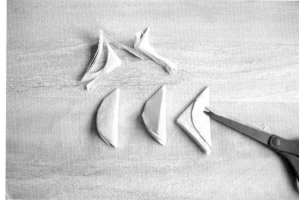

How-To:

1. Fold the cocktail napkin in half to form a triangle, then fold it in half two more times to form a smaller triangle.

2. Trim the edge into a petal shape, leaving the folded point attached.

3. Unfold and pull the four layers apart. Arrange the layers to form a flower.

4. Fold and hold the center of the flower.

5. Twist the center firmly to form a tip to hold the layers together.

6. Fluff the petals and repeat these steps until all of your flowers complete.

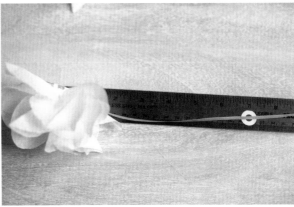

7. Cut 13 stands of ribbon 6 feet long each.

8. Adhere the first flower onto the ribbon with the round reinforcement label. To do this, place the twisted tip of the flower inside of the circle and fold the label over to hold the bloom on to the ribbon.

9. Measure 7 inches and add another label. There should be eight flowers per ribbon.

10. Tie the end of the finished floral ribbon to a wooden dowel, stick, or metal rod.

We Are One

Photography: Knot & Pop
Main Hero Shot: Gary Didsbury
Style/Concept: Knot & Pop
Paper Decorations: Knot & Pop and Sarah
Louise Matthews

Knot & Pop creates dynamic projects for
those that want to celebrate in unique and
imaginative ways. This flower was a piece
from "We Are One," a compelling private
dining experience made to transform an
everyday setting into an intimate and
incredible experience.

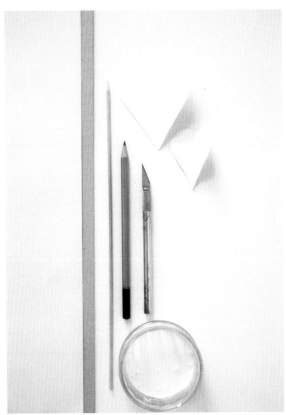

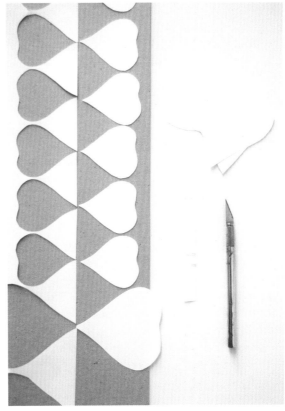

Materials:

- Standard weight paper
- Pencil
- Scissors or box cutter
- PVA glue
- Bamboo skewer

How-To:

1. Create two heart shapes, one a roughly third bigger than the other. Ensure you have a symmetrical shape. These will form the templates for your petals.

2. To make one flower, cut out the following: 6x of each size petal; a circle of paper (size of a 10 pence); a 5 cm strip of paper and fringe.

3. Curl the pointed end of the petal round a pencil towards you and the wide end of the petal away from you. This will give the flower a 3D shape.

4. Using your paper circle as a base, layering one on top of another, glue your larger petals clockwise to make a flower head.

5. Repeat this process with the smaller petals.

6. Roll your fringed strip of paper into a stamen.

7. Glue the stamen to the central of the flower and tease out the fringing.

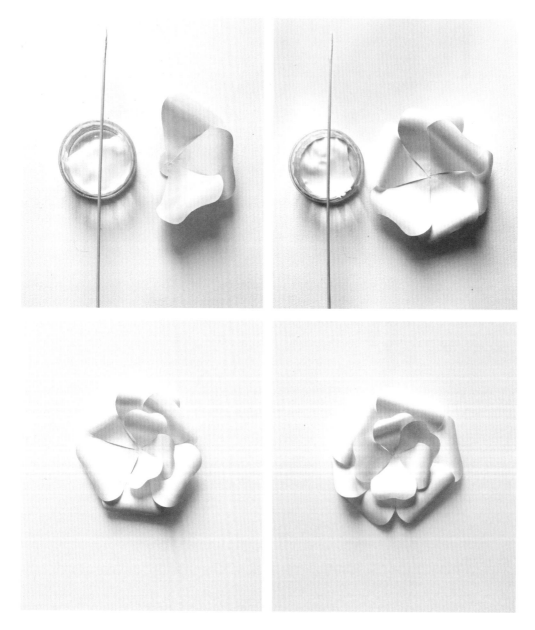

Use your flowers to create a mass installation such as the heart below, or pop them on sticks and into vases. Experiment with colour, pattern or even the texture to make your paper flowers work for your event.

Paper Rose Wedding Bouquet

Design: Lia Griffith
Crafting: Lia Griffith
Photography: Lia Griffith

This bouquet is a gorgeous way to add a little personal touch to your wedding. Adding these elegant paper roses to the mix will help create an event that is unique and memorable. This version of Lia's paper rose includes three tones of pink, peach and blush. The watercolor print on both sides creates a visual texture and adds a painterly touch. If you are not planning a wedding, no problem! This lovely bouquet is a great Mother's Day gift or a sculptural bouquet to dress your table.

Materials:

- Scissors
- Hot glue gun
- Floral wire
- Floral tape
- 2 yards of ribbon

How-To:

1. Download and print the 18 paper rose PDFs and two sheets of the leaf PDFs onto letter paper. The PDFs each have two pages, one to print on the front of the paper and the other to print on the back. This double-sided printing works best printed with a laser printer. (link: http://liagriffith.com/diy-paper-rose-wedding-bouquet/)

You can also create your own template. For each rose you will need two 5-petaled flowers of a 3.75" diameter, one 4-petaled flower, one 3-petaled flower, and three separate petals of the same size as the petals on your flowers (about 2"). Each flower should have a small tab on the edge of one of the edge petals (see image). You will also need 3" leaves with stems between .25" and .5". You can mimic the look of the PDF template with specialty colored paper.

2. Use the edge of the blade of a pair of scissors to curl two corners of petals and the edges of a leaf. Fold the leaf in half.

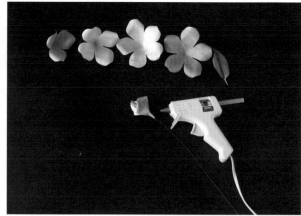

4. Glue the edge tabs of petals 4-6 to their opposite petal to form them into cones.

5. Fold 1" of the floral wire and glue to edge of petal 1.

6. Roll petal around the wire center then curl back one edge.

7. Glue the bottom tip of petal 2 to petal 1 and wrap it around, adjusting the curled edges as needed.

8. Repeat with petal 3, rotating the petal to form the look of the rose center.

9. Skewer petals 4-7 onto the wire stem and glue each one to center base.

10. Glue the stem of the leaf into the floral.

11. Use floral tape to wrap stems of the leaf and rose, stretching the tape to activate the sticky gum.

12. Repeat these steps to create 18 roses and 24 leaves.

13. Hold the base of the bouquet with one hand and form a round dome with flowers, adding leaves between each rose.

14. Wrap the base of the bouquet with floral tape, then wrap downward to cover half of the stem in tape.

15. Fold each wire up towards bouquets, on wire at a time, to create a thicker handle and more finished end.

16. Cover all but the very end of stems with floral tape.

17. Wrap ribbon around the handle, starting at the top and leaving an extra 10'' at each end for a bow. Wrap to the end of the stem then back up again.

18. Use the extra 10" of ribbon to tie a bow at the base of the bouquet.

Valentine's Day Wreath

Design: Brittany Watson Jepsen
Crafting: Brittany Watson Jepsen
Photography: Trisha Zemp

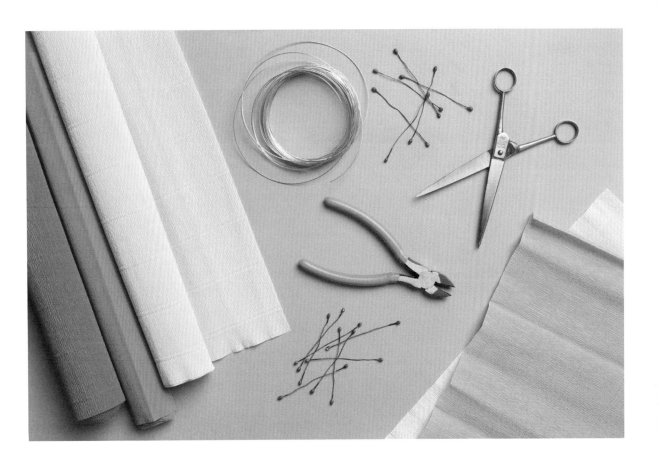

Materials:

- Scissors

- Wire cutters

- Wire

- Crepe paper in shades of pinks and whites

- Any type of flower pattern (daffodils as an example)

- Glue gun

How-To:

The circle:

1. Form a circle with your wire. Size it to the shape of your head, allowing about 5 extra inches.

2. Wind these 5 extra inches around the circle shape as many times as possible.

3. Cut a piece of crepe paper about 1"thick and about 3' in length going against the grain of the crepe paper. Folding the paper first will help this go faster.

4. Use your thumbs to stretch the entire length of the crepe paper.

5. Glue the ends of the paper together and start tightly winding it around the wire.

6. Glue the end piece down tightly when you reach the end of the wire.

Make your flowers:

Any crepe paper flower will work for this project, or you can check the designer's blog for her daffodil tutorial (http://www.thehousethatlarsbuilt.com/2014/01/how-to-make-paper-flower-daffodil.html). Give any flower you make a stem of about 4"-5".

To attach the flowers:

1. Wrap the stem of your first flower around the wire circle as many times as possible. Leave about 1" of space between the flower and the wire so it will be easy to adjust the flower later if you need to.

2. Place the second flower next to the first and wrap the stem the same way.

3. Continue adding flowers until they are evenly spaced all the way around the crown. The designer used 9 daffodils for hers.

4. To fill in any gaps, cut crepe paper leaves (with the grain of the paper going vertically) and glue them to the stems of the flowers.

Paper Flower Crown

Design: Alana Jones-Mann
Crafting: Alana Jones-Mann
Photography: Alana Jones-Mann

Materials:

- Assortment of bright colored paper or hand-painted paper
- Scissors
- Hot glue gun
- Floral wire - thin and medium gauge
- Floral tape (optional)

How-To:

1. Download and print the flower template (link: http://blog.fossil.com/files/2014/03/Flower_template1.pdf), or create your own template for a five-petaled flower 3.75" in diameter. Leave a gap between two petals and a small tab at the edge of one of the petals next to the gap.

2. Cut the petals for your flowers. For each flower you will need 7 to 10 individual petals (#5 on the web template, or the petal opposite the tabbed petal on your own template), one flower without the #5 petal, and two flowers with all of their petals.

3. To assemble the individual petals, glue your first individual petal to a 6" piece of thin-gauge floral wire and wrap it around the wire to create the center of the flower.

4. Use the flat edge of your scissors to curl the edges of the other individual petals and attach each one to the stem using hot glue.

5. Once all of the individual petals have been added, move on to the remaining cut-out flowers. Curl the edges of each of your remaining pieces and close each flower by gluing the edge.

6. String the flowers over the wire and up the stem, then apply hot glue to the base between each cut-out one at a time. Push the flower against the base to make sure it adheres. Work with the four-petaled flower first, then the two five-petaled flowers.

7. Lastly, fix any flower petals that need additional curling or trimming.

8. Take your medium gauge floral wire and shape it into a circle that fits comfortably on your head. Double this circle to make the crown a bit sturdier.

9. Add each of your flowers on to the crown by wrapping the wire stems around the wire base.

10. Once you are happy with the look of the crown, it's ready to wear!

Flower Headband

Design: By Madeline Trait
Crafting: By Madeline Trait
Photography: By Madeline Trait

Add some fun flowers to your celebration with festive flower headbands. Make an activity out of it so you and your guests can each create your own unique headband. Play around with the placement of your headband, as it will look great worn many different ways. Now you are ready to party!

Materials:

- Glue gun
- Crepe paper (multiple colors)
- Ribbon (multiple colors)
- Dried pods, berries, and/or buttons
- Wire

How-To:

1. Grab your crepe paper and cut it into 2" wide strips. Be sure to cut parallel to the creases of the paper. Then cut each 2" wide strip into 2" x 2" squares.

2. Cut the corners of one end of the square to give it the shape of a petal.

3. Gently stretch the end of the squre with cut edges to give it more of a petal shape.

4. Make the center of the flower. Cut a piece of wire about 4" long, then make a small loop at one end. Bend the end of the loop so it is perpendicular to the rest of the wire. It should look like an upside down L. Then use your glue gun to glue your button or dried pod to the loop.

5. Put a line of glue on the unstretched end of a petal. This will be the end you glue to the bottom of the flower center.

6. Glue the petals on to the flower center one at a time, using an accordion fold and layering the petals as you go. Repeat this step, layering the petals as you go. You can adjust petal size and quantity for bigger or smaller flower.

7. Cut the excess wire that is creating the stem of your flower. Now the flowers are ready to be glued to the ribbon (headband). Be sure to try on your headband as you build it! Your head is curved and the flowers may lay differently on your head vs. the table.

8. Add additional adornments such as the dried pods, buttons, dried seeds, etc. to fill in the gaps between flowers.

Fruit Leather Cake Flowers

Cake: Wild Orchid Baking Company
Crafting: Wild Orchid Baking Company
Photography: Mark Davidson

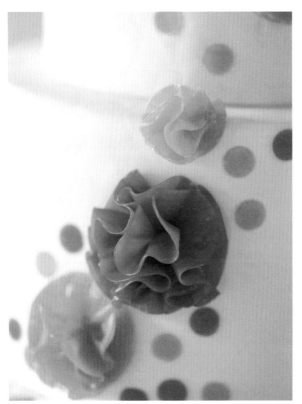

Materials:

- Fruit leather
- Round cookie cutters
- Small bowl of water
- Small paint brush
- Floral wire (tooth picks or skewers would work as well)
- Piece of foam

How-To:

1. Using a round cookie cutter, cut circles out of the fruit leather. The size of the cutter you use will determine how large of a puff you have at the end. For these puffs Wild Orchid Baking Company used round cutters that were 1/2" to 2" in diameter.

2. Pick up a fruit leather round, and using your thumbs and forefingers, press the sides of the round together towards the center of the circle. You'll end up with a shape resembling a ruffled "x". Be sure to press toward the center of the circle so you don't close the "x" entirely. The open loops are what give the puff it's shape.

3. If your fruit leather begins to dry out, brush a small amount of water over the individual ruffles to help them stick together. Add more ruffles until you achieve the desired puff shape. Set formed puff onto a piece of styrofoam. Use floral wires or toothpicks to prop the puffs into the desired shape and allow them to dry overnight. The wires or toothpicks will help to keep the puffs from drooping or loosing their shape as they dry. You may need to allow them to dry longer depending on the humidity.

4. Add dots to your cake or cupcake design by cutting out small circles from the leftover fruit leather. Apply using royal icing or water, just like the puffs. Apply to a finished cake using small dots of royal icing, or if applying to fondant just brush on a small amount of water where you'd like the puff to stick.

For cupcakes: Set onto freshly piped frosting.

INDEX

By Madeline Trait

www.madelinetrait.com

By Madeline Trait is what emerged from Madeline Trait's passion for good design, crafty spirit, and can-do attitude.

Madeline started her career in architectural and interior design, which equipped her with the skills to conceptualize and visualize space, think outside the box, and find creative solutions. However, she was always happiest when she was working with flowers, sketching, conceptualizing new ideas, and making all those ideas in her head come to life. So in 2009 Madeline gave into her creative musings and decided to open her own design studio.

P.042 - 045, 226 - 227

——

Cakegirls

thecakegirls.com

Cakegirls are Mary and Brenda Maher, sisters that were born and raised in Rochester, Michigan. As adults, they both spent time working at a bakery in Detroit, Michigan and rediscovered their passion for creating cakes for weddings and other special occasions. Their time in Detroit convinced the sisters they could do better with their own business in Chicago, and thus Cakegirls was born as an online store for people who love to make cakes and throw parties. Mary and Brenda have gathered some of their favorite tips and tricks to help you make the cake and throw the party!

P.150 - 153

——

Chelsea Foy

lovelyindeed.com

Chelsea Foy is the maker behind *Lovely Indeed,* a DIY and lifestyle blog about all of the lovely things in life. Her work has been featured on *Apartment Therapy, Buzzfeed, HGTV,* and more. She recently co-authored *Make Your Day,* a digital crafting book. Chelsea resides in Los Angeles, California with her husband, where they spend their time exploring, adventuring, and looking for the best tacos in town.

P.046 - 049, 086 - 087

——

Claire Cassidy

southbynorth.net

Claire loves photography, styling, and crafting, and in her spare time runs the blog *South by North.* She is originally from London, and now lives in sunny Sydney.

P.184 - 187

——

Dani Altamura

www.highwallsblog.com

Dani Altamura is an Australian blogger with a desire to inspire. She is a lover of simple things: minimalist design, use of negative space, and pops of vibrant colors. Her blog, *High Walls,* is a creative lifestyle blog showcasing DIY and craft projects, delicious recipes, design, and style inspiration. Dani believes in living a creative and inspired lifestyle and hopes to share this with her readers.

P.024 - 027, 084 - 085

——

Eleanna Kotsikou

pinterest.com/zdropz/

Eleanna Kotsikou, aka Z drop, comes from Greece. She has lived in France, Italy, the Netherlands and the UK, but she's never traveled outside Europe. She has studied architecture and urbanism. The creative process from concept to end result is really important for her. Eleanna loves color and design. She dances and she laughs (too) loud.

P.174 - 183

——

Fanfan Yang

fanfanyang.com

Fanfan Yang is a visual artist and jewelry designer. Her obsession with life's little fragments drives her to collect ordinary materials and turn them into something else. After graduating from UAL in London, she now works in New York.

P.188 - 191

——

Gardenista

www.gardenista.com

Erin Boyle is the associate editor at *Gardenista: Sourcebook for Cultivated Living.* Erin lives in Brooklyn, NY where she does her best to carve out a tiny growing space in two window boxes and a sill full of houseplants.

P.060 - 063

Gloribell Lebrón

www.knowhowshedoesit.com

Gloribell Lebrón is an interior designer with an ample background in graphic design. She runs a blog called *I Don't Know How She Does It.* She is passionate about design and styling beautiful yet livable spaces.

P.108 - 111, 118 - 121

Hannah Hathaway

www.welivedhappilyeverafter.com

Hannah Hathaway is a DIY enthusiast and graphic art-loving Marine wife and momma. When she isn't busy having fun with the love of her life and their adorable little girl, she spends her time blogging about military life, graphic design, photo editing, and her passion for creative crafting around the home. Her blog is called *We Lived Happily Ever After.*

P.146 - 149

Janelle Nicole Wylie

www.lavendersfloral.com

Janelle Nicole Wylie is an artist who applies her knowledge of complimentary colors, texture, and 3D design to all of her arrangements. They are not simply decorations to adorn a table or compliment a beautiful bride; instead, each arrangement exists as a canvas on its own. She sees the beauty in nature and strives to create works that allow others to see the world as she does. When she is not creating, she is seeking inspiration through other means. She loves to spend time outdoors and travel, and always makes sure she finds time to marvel over the setting sun. Janelle is more than a conventional florist; she paints a masterpiece with the placement of every flower.

P.016 - 019

Justine Hand

designskool.net

Justine Hand is a New England native and historic house buff. She lives in Newton where she is working to restore her own historic home. Justine writes the design blog *Design Skool,* which is founded on the belief that your home should reflect your story, your history, and your heritage.

P.074 - 075

Karla Lim

ohsoverypretty.com

Karla Lim is a calligrapher, crafter, and a lover of all things pretty. She is a co-blogger of *Oh So Very Pretty,* a DIY, craft, and design blog that features projects for decorating your home, designing your events and creating unique gifts. She is passionate about the art of writing, and runs a calligraphy and design studio called Written Word. If she's not home working on her crafting or paper projects, she is out exploring and travelling in the beautiful city of Vancouver.

P.050 - 055

Kelly S. Rowe

livelaughrowe.com

Kelly S. Rowe is an Etsy shop owner and blogger based out of St. Louis, MO. Kelly is the content creator and author of *Live Laugh Rowe,* a creative lifestyle blog. There you will find a collaboration of crafting tutorials, DIY projects, recipes, inspirational stories, travel, and more. She loves to spend time in her craft room and kitchen creating content for her readers, photography, walking her fur babies, and traveling with her husband.

———

Kindred

yaykindred.com

"Kindred," by definition, means "sharing in the same spirit, belief, attitude or feeling" — and Kindred wants your experience with them to be nothing short of this. Kindred isn't just working with you; Kindred wants to show you that the dreaming and creating process can be every bit as fun as the end result itself. For Kindred, there are very few things more thrilling than the concept phase. Kindred lives to see what could be and thrives on figuring out how to make it happen. Wherever you are in the process, share your wildest ideas and most unrefined dreams with Kindred; Kindred will love it, nourish it and cultivate it to unimaginable proportions resulting in an event, product or experience that Kindred partnered to create. And that's why "kindred" is so important to their team; it's not just the way they work — it's who Kindred is.

———

Knot & Pop

www.knotandpop.com

Knot & Pop is Claire Knill and Susie Young, a duo that offers a distinctive, creative touch to wedding scheming and theming as they recognize that everyone, every couple, every occasion is different – therefore every event should be too.

Couples come to Knot & Pop for unique, hand-crafted, meticulously sourced and precisely delivered events that make big day occasions truly special, and create interest and engage guests at every step.

Knot & Pop events encompass a sense of spirit and fun, with a fresh and modern approach to give clients their day, in the most unique way.

With careers in fashion PR and marketing and the luxury travel industry, the duo has worked at award-winning brands such as ASOS and Black Tomato, where they applied their creative and obsessive organizational skills to a career's worth of events and launches for both private and brand clients.

———

Lexy Ward

theproperpinwheel.com

Lexy Ward is the founder, editor, and stylist behind the DIY blog *The Proper Pinwheel*. She has a passion for all things entertaining and lives to inspire others to create. She can usually be found with a hot glue gun in one hand and a Diet Coke in the other. She currently resides in Denver, Colorado with her husband and daughter.

———

Lia Griffith

liagriffith.com

Lia Griffith is a daily DIYer, designer, photographer, stylist, creative inventor, and big dreamer. She lives a handcrafted life and created her blog of the same name to share it with you, to inspire you, to help you remember that creative genius lives inside of all of you. Whether you are looking for decorating ideas, a DIY paper flower, or a gift wrap idea, *Lia Griffith* is the right place!

———

Lily & May

www.lilyandmay.co.uk

Lily & May is an award-winning Essex-based floral wedding design company with a love for creating romantic and whimsical designs that are influenced by color and texture.

The team strives to produce beautiful wedding flowers for your day and works closely with the client during the design process. Their approach is completely bespoke, leading to weddings that perfectly reflect their client's style and personality.

———

Lucy Akins

www.craftberrybush.com

Because Lucy grew up in a family of musicians and artists, she learned at an early age the beauty art can bring to one's life. She wanted her children to have the same experience and so the journey began. She built her blog, *Craftberry Bush,* to share not only her creations, but her family's own personal journey. Lucy hopes it can inspire others to put aside their fears and hesitations and enjoy the beauty art has to offer.

———

Maggie Mao

www.maggiemaostudio.com

Maggie Mao is a Shanghai-based florist and designer. She has been working with some of the finest florists in New York since graduating from FIT. Her work evokes nature with sophistication and elegance.

———

Marilyn and Kaleb Nimz

www.brewedtogether.com

Brewed Together was created by husband and wife bloggers Kaleb and Marilyn Nimz on January 1, 2013 as a New Year's resolution in order to share their creative work and adventures. The inspirations for and focuses of the blog include their collaborative interests: travel, photography, fashion, graphic design, handmade projects, cooking and baking, cycling, running, and any outdoor adventure!

———

Mathilde heart Manech

www.mathildeheartmanech.com

Mathilde heart Manech is a happy lifestyle blog, written by freelance writer and blogger Lisa Murdoch. Her little space on the internet includes all the things that make Lisa smile: great design, contemporary craft, fashion, and positive thoughts.

———

Michelle Edgemont

www.michelleedgemont.com

Michelle Edgemont is a Brooklyn, NY-based event designer who specializes in handmade custom décor. She frequently produces DIY projects for HGTV, *Green Wedding Shoes, The Knot,* and books. She teaches craft classes in New York City and has spoken at many business conferences such as Making Things Happen and Altitude Summit.

———

Pollen Floral Design

www.bostonpollen.com

Pollen Floral Design focuses on using seasonal, high quality blooms to create beautiful, fresh designs unique to your wedding or gathering. Pollen designs are inspired by natural elements and textures to reflect a lush, garden aesthetic.

———

Rachel Mae Smith

thecraftedlife.com

Rachel Mae Smith lives and crafts in San Francisco, CA. She loves doable DIY projects and strives to make crafting easy and fun over on her blog, The Crafted Life. When she's not pinning pictures or brushing glitter out of her hair, you can find her exploring and photographing the Bay Area.

P.088 - 089

—

Razzle Dazzle Rose

www.razzledazzlerose.co.uk

Online stationery supplier Razzle Dazzle Rose specializes in recycled and eco-friendly stationery and giftware. It is the ideal solution if you want to create cards and wedding stationery on a budget.

Since the company's establishment in January 2012, business owner Sharon Langsdale has won awards for creativity and design and has been a panelist for national craft magazine titles.

P.192 - 195

—

Russell Brown

pokeacupuncture.com

After graduating from the University of California, Berkeley with a degree in journalism, Russell Brown came home to Los Angeles and worked in the film industry for several years. He was out at breakfast one day when he overheard a woman at the neighboring table talk about enrolling in acupuncture school. It was like a door had opened, and he knew he was being prompted to reprioritize his life and dedicate himself to the betterment of others. Russell went down to the school and enrolled the next day. After graduating from acupuncture school, Russell worked in several clinics, and finally opened his own, Poke Acupuncture.

P.122 - 125

—

Sharon Garofalow

www.cupcakesandcutlery.com

Sharon Garofalow is the creator of *CupcakesAndCutlery. com*, a life and style blog all about defining your personal style and sharing it in everything you do. She is a mom to two amazing little boys and married to the raddest man in all the land. The blog is a place to find out how Sharon and her family live a casual, California cool lifestyle. Sharon loves to share her creativity through craft tutorials, inspired entertaining ideas, and recipes, as well as share her favorite products, from kids' toys to home decor and fashion for the whole family. This warm weather-loving girl loves girls' weekend trips, trying new restaurants, and watching reality television.

P.164 - 167

—

Sheryl Yen

www.ohsoverypretty.com

Sheryl Yen is one of two voices behind *Oh So Very Pretty*, a DIY and food blog created to share their love of all things pretty. Sheryl is a marketing maven who is inspired by music, food, travel, and the outdoors. She currently resides in beautiful Vancouver, British Columbia and loves to explore the city with her fiancé, family, and friends. She is passionate about sharing her love of finding beauty in everyday ordinary things and hopes to share that love with others.

P.070 - 073

—

SoulMakes

www.soulmakes.com

SoulMakes is collaboration between two love birds, MacKenzie and Trevor Mars. She is the designer, maker and photographer behind this collection of wild and free accessories and he is the visionary that breathed life into their passionate story, with his business and tech-savvy skills. Together they share a bohemian wonderland, where they hope you'll find your hidden treasure.

With designs that appeal to all free spirits, their collection is inspired by all things worldly, capturing a little of the Wild West, a bit of gypsy magic, and a whole lot of soul. Each piece is carefully handcrafted and adorned with unique details.

P.140 - 145

Stephanie Brubaker

www.stephmodo.com

Stephanie Brubaker is the Seattle-based lifestyle blogger behind the blog Stephmodo, where she talks about all things both practical and pretty. When she is not making something special in the kitchen, exploring her favorite local hot spots, or dreaming up her next party, Stephanie daydreams of going to France with her husband and four children to revisit their recently renovated cottage.

P.100 - 103

Trish

www.underlockandkeyblog.com

Trish (Tricia MacK) is the writer of the blog *Under Lock and Key,* where she shares posts about crafting, cooking, baking and motherhood. She lives on the north shore of Sydney, Australia with her husband, son, and their little sausage dog.

P.094 - 099, 114 - 117, 154 - 157

Urbanic

www.urbanicpaper.com

Urbanic is a niche boutique dedicated to all things paper. The shop has a reputation for its unique greeting cards, beautiful letterpress items, stylish papers, modern gifts, office accessories, and custom stationery. It's frequented by design lovers and event planners throughout Los Angeles and beyond.

P.104 - 107

Whitney Curtis

www.hellowhitneycurtis.com

Whitney Curtis is a blogger by profession and by hobby. She freelanced, blogged, networked, DIY-ed, photographed, and blogged some more. All that led her to her current job as Senior Editor of *The Home Depot's Apron Blog.* On her own blog, *The Curtis Casa,* Whitney likes to keep it light and fun. There are projects from around her house, a little bit about gardening, a little bit about style, and lots of fun things from the internet.

P.066 - 069

Wild Orchid Baking Company

www.wildorchidbaking.com

Wild Orchid Baking Company is a custom cake studio located on the coast of New Hampshire, serving New Hampshire, Maine, Massachusetts and beyond. It started as a side project for chef Erin, creating cakes for friends, family and fellow chefs out of her home kitchen. After a career in fine dining as the pastry chef at Boston's Locke Ober and the regionally acclaimed Bedford Village Inn, Erin decided it was time to go out on her own and Wild Orchid Baking Co. was born!

Design and flavor possibilities are limitless, and each cake is as special and unique as the person it is for. Wild Orchid Baking Company's goal is to create gorgeous confections that taste as amazing as they look.

P.228 - 232

ACKNOWLEDGEMENTS

We would like to extend our gratitude to the artists and designers who have contributed generously to this publication. We are also grateful to those whose names are not mentioned in the credits but have provided their assistance and support. Last but not least, thanks goes to the people who put together this book — it would not have been possible without your innovation and creativity. Our team includes editor Jill Guo and designer Irma Zuo, to whom we are truly grateful.